The Paradox of Disability

D0878055

The Paradox of Disability

Responses to Jean Vanier and
L'Arche Communities from
Theology and the Sciences

Edited by

Hans S. Reinders

WILLIAM B. EERDMANS PUBLISHING COMPANY

GRAND RAPIDS, MICHIGAN / CAMBRIDGE, U.K.

© 2010 Wm. B. Eerdmans Publishing Co.

Published 2010 by
Wm. B. Eerdmans Publishing Co.
2140 Oak Industrial Drive N.E., Grand Rapids, Michigan 49505 /
P.O. Box 163, Cambridge CB3 9PU U.K.

Printed in the United States of America

16 15 14 13 12 11 10   7 6 5 4 3 2 1

Library of Congress Cataloging-in-Publication Data

The paradox of disability: responses to Jean Vanier and L'Arche communities
    from theology and the sciences /
    edited by Hans S. Reinders.
        p.   cm.
Based on papers originally presented at a conference held in Trosly-Breuil, France
    in March 2007.
ISBN 978-0-8028-6511-3 (pbk.: alk. paper)
1. Church work with the developmentally disabled — Congresses.
2. Vanier, Jean, 1928 — Congresses.   3. Arche (Association) — Congresses.
4. Developmentally disabled — Congresses.   I. Reinders, Hans S.

BV4461.3.W43   2010
205'.697 — dc22

                                                              2010013888

www.eerdmans.com

Contents

v

Acknowledgments

This book came out of a project that was initiated by the John Templeton Foundation in Philadelphia and named the Humble Approach Initiative. The foundation asked Xavier Le Pichon and me to chair a conference on the question of what there is to learn from people with disabilities. The conference eventually took place in the village of Trosly-Breuil in northern France in March 2007, where we were hosted by the community of L'Arche.

The contributors to this volume wish to express their gratitude to the John Templeton Foundation, whose support, particularly in the person of Mary Ann Meyers, the executive director of the project, made this book possible. We are also grateful to the people of L'Arche, whose presence made the event much more than just another academic gathering. We wish to express a special word of appreciation to Jean Vanier, the founder of this community, for not only hosting us but also for his participation in our proceedings, which was an enriching experience.

As we bring these fond memories to mind, it was with all the more poignant sadness that we learned of the tragic death of Dr. Christopher Newell, our Australian colleague, whom some of us have known for many years as a friend. As the reader can see from the table of contents, Christopher's essay is the final one in this volume, and it turned out to be his last finished paper. Rereading this essay, which in many ways expresses the magnitude of the problem of academic discourse in the presence of disability, one becomes painfully aware of how gifted people like Christopher must constantly battle to live the life to which they aspire with as serious an impairing condition as he had. His battle is over. *Requiescat in pace.*

PART I

Introduction

Human Vulnerability:
A Conversation at L'Arche

Hans S. Reinders

The Occasion

This volume is the result of a conversation held by its contributors in Trosly-Breuil, France, in March 2007. The village is known as the hometown of the community of L'Arche, where people with and without intellectual disabilities live and work together.[1] Since the theme of our meeting was the question of what we can learn from people with disabilities, Trosly-Breuil suggested itself as a suitable place to meet. L'Arche is a spiritual community inspired by and built on the Beatitudes, which Jesus enunciated in the Gospels of Matthew and Luke. It is intended to be a place where people who have been marginalized by society are accepted. The community of L'Arche is a celebration of difference in that it brings together not only people with various gifts but also people from various cultural and religious traditions.

The question of what there is to learn from people with disabilities can

---

1. L'Arche is French for "the Ark." Founded by Jean Vanier and Fr. Thomas Philippe in 1964, L'Arche is an international movement of residential communities in thirty-four countries worldwide. In L'Arche homes people with intellectual disabilities (known as core people, or "core members") live in community with their caregivers (known as "assistants"). L'Arche honors individuals as a sign of *agape* and mutual respect. In the United States, L'Arche communities often exist on a financial shoestring. Besides receiving room and board, assistants may live on a few hundred dollars per month. The earthy reality of life together is punctuated by deep spiritual commitments and experiences. L'Arche is a Christian movement that embraces other traditions.

no doubt be approached in any number of ways, but for reasons that will become apparent, it was a salutary decision to discuss it in the context of this extraordinary place. As it is expressed in the writings of Jean Vanier — and is confirmed by the charter of the Communities of L'Arche — its first and foremost goal is to build community. Due to discontent with the liberal individualism of our time, we often hear "community" spoken of in endearing terms — at least in the Western world — as a place where people positively experience the social nature of being human. As we learned from our experiences at L'Arche, the truth of the matter is quite different. More than anything else, "community" marks the experience of the brokenness of human beings. Very often L'Arche attracts people who want to share the lives of people with disabilities in order to make the world a better place. But those who have spent years of their lives in one of its communities know better. As Vanier has explained many times, there is no way of doing something *for* other people if you do not first learn how to receive whatever gift *they* have to offer, which presupposes your willingness to accept that you also are a person in need. The L'Arche community is about learning to receive other people as God's gift.

Before introducing the various contributions of this book to its readers, let me pause to reflect on how being hosted by such a community has affected our discussions about the drafts of original papers. The people who were invited by the Templeton Foundation to contribute are academics from a variety of disciplines. Together they, too, represent a kind of community — the "scientific community." But as we all know, the scientific community frequently turns out to be a community of division rather than a community celebrating mutual receptivity. While the university — in its original idea — was planned and designed to bring people of all disciplines together in order to reflect the universe of learning, nowadays it is much more often a place of competing departments and contesting paradigms and methodologies. There is no better way to explain the current demand for interdisciplinary study in academic circles than by pointing to the apparent lack of understanding and appreciation of what professionals in fields other than one's own are doing. In many departments this even holds true for people in one's own discipline.

As was to be expected, our first round of discussions in Trosly-Breuil provided ample testimony to this state of affairs. Those among us who represented the sciences seemed to wonder whether people from other disciplines — particularly theology — had any regard at all for the basic rules of science, such as, for example, the rule of building theory on sound evidence. The theologians, in turn, wondered how scientists manage again and again to turn a blind eye to the metaphysical underpinnings of their scientific beliefs.

The irony of this situation is that the meeting that produced this book was organized in the context of the Templeton Foundation's Humble Approach Initiative. Whatever the qualities and qualifications that academics bring to scientific meetings, humility is rarely one of them. Despite the fact that we were hosted by a spiritual community where people learn to receive one another as a gift, the question of what we can learn from people with disabilities presented itself initially as the next opportunity for an intellectual standoff on the battlefield called "modern science."

As our meeting proceeded, however, things turned out to be slightly different. What was doomed to become a perfect example of performative contradiction turned into an exercise of performative reflection. That is to say, the way our discussions proceeded gradually tuned in to their subject matter. What they were about was reflected in how they were conducted: they changed from contest into conversation. As academics, we are often trained in thinking that our own field best explains the way things are in the world. Rarely are we encouraged to learn about the limitations of our knowledge. This is quite strange. It is only because of its limited scope that scientific method produces any knowledge at all. And it is only by recognizing the limitations of the kind of knowledge our own field produces that we can learn to appreciate difference, and thus understand what the scientific community is about.

Our meeting in Trosly-Breuil was in this respect clearly under the influence of Jean Vanier's participation. Carefully listening and responding to the papers at hand, he showed us that the task was to find each person's way of making a contribution. While reflecting on what we can learn from people with disabilities can go in many different directions, our way, guided by the spirituality of L'Arche, came to regard our very different approaches to this question as an exercise in inclusion. A truly human community is not only about unity and wholeness; it is also about learning to live with difference and limitation, which holds for the scientific community as well. Once we understand this, we can learn to see that claims to unity and wholeness are really impositions by means of which particularized perspectives usurp the world of human experience and blind us to the variety of what there is to see.

Vanier's understanding of living with people who embody brokenness as a way of building human community is a perfect illustration of this insight. Of course, the brokenness and limitations of people with disabilities — particularly intellectual disabilities — is too evident to be overlooked. Much less clear, however, is that, in looking at them in this way, we may fail to see or own brokenness and limitations. To look at other people's brokenness and limitation without seeing our own is a gesture of power; to acknowledge our own brokenness and limitation in the face of theirs is a gesture of community. In this regard L'Arche is an extraordinary place of learning.

In order to show how our discussions in Trosly-Breuil have been affected by its gestures of community, I have ordered the contributions to this volume in a particular way. As I have noted above, according to Vanier, "community" is not about trying to live a shared ideal; rather, it is about learning the truth about oneself and others. Contrary to a frequent misreading of its experience, L'Arche has nothing to do with an ideal community that is shaped by morally exceptional people. Instead, it has everything to do with people learning to be with each other and be accepted as who and what they are. Thus understood, learning to live in L'Arche is not about following a pattern or a plan according to which the moral self must be shaped. Its gestures of community are about accepting brokenness and limitation in order to create the freedom of celebrating difference.

This insight immediately affects the way we answer the question of what we can learn from people with disabilities. This question has been answered frequently in terms of some kind of capacity that has been attributed to them. Very often that capacity is of a moral kind, such that the people possessing it are recommended as moral exemplars. People with physical disabilities, for example, report that they are frequently praised for their capacity of enduring suffering. People with intellectual disability — also referred to as "mental handicap," "learning disability," or "developmental disability" — are commended for their uncomplicated approach to life, which in past times earned them the pet name of "holy innocents."

In more recent times, people with disabilities have rejected all such qualifications because they do not want to be qualified in ways that make them exceptional. While many of their lives do not fit the stories of horror and disaster that are told about them, their lives are equally misrepresented by stories of praise and blessing. All these people want is to be seen as simply human — no more and no less. If we accept this demand, as I suggest we should, there will be no single answer to the question of what we can learn from people with disabilities. As a matter of fact, we may learn many different things from them, depending on who they are and what their lives are like, and also depending on who we are and what our lives are like.

This fact of inevitable diversity is reflected in the essays brought together in this volume. However, despite the many different ways in which we approach our question, there are also overlapping issues and similar thoughts. This is particularly clear if we read these essays as responses to Jean Vanier's reflections, someone who has shared most of his life with people with disabilities. For that reason, this book takes its point of departure in his account of what he has learned from living and working in L'Arche. Therefore, his essay will appear at the very beginning of this volume as the calling initiative, so to speak. The logic of ordering the papers in this volume shows how the call to respond to Vanier's account and the issues it raises can be heard in many different ways. Each of the contributors picks up themes and thoughts that elicit a response from her or his own particular research projects.

The Essays

In considering what he believes is the raison d'être of L'Arche, Vanier recalls his first experience of looking at the faces of the men who lived in an institution for people with learning disabilities where his friend Father Thomas Philippe was chaplain. Written on their faces was a cry: "Do you love me? Am I important? Will you be my friend?" According to Vanier, the experiment of L'Arche began as the response to that cry.

It is to this subject of love as a fundamental "need" that Stephen Post's essay responds. His focus oscillates between the love given in the process of care and the love received as a return. Post compares the nature of the response Vanier has given with the one he has found in the work of Tom Kitwood, who is known in the United Kingdom as well as in North America for his "dementia care mapping." According to Post, what Vanier says about his work with people with disabilities resembles what Kitwood says about his work with people with Alzheimer's disease. Post finds in their views the resources to support his objection to what he calls "hypercognitivism," the notion that the key to our humanity resides in our cognitive faculties. Against this notion, Post argues, our humanity is constituted by "other-regarding" love. Only other-regarding love can be truly universal in that it addresses the basic need that, according to Vanier, all human beings have, which is the need to be nurtured by love and to be accepted as valuable.

The communities of L'Arche are spiritual communities, as Vanier explains, and they have taught him the need for prayer and spirituality — "not only for people with disabilities, but for everybody." This claim raises important questions about the meaning of spiritual practices for people whose personality is at least partially characterized by cognitive impairment. However, Vanier does not think that that is a serious problem, because they communicate "through their bodily gestures and simple words of love, or of anger." In Vanier's understanding, their spirituality is very much about communication, which appears from the fact that they celebrate whatever gifts there are to thank God for. The gestures of rejoicing can be shared, if not always in words.

This same claim about the meaning of spirituality appears as the central focus of Christina Puchalski's paper, but within a different context. She reviews the literature on the importance of spiritual care for the quality of life of people with dementia. Her analysis shows how spirituality and religion are supportive in this specific context, which is characterized by a *progressive* loss of mental functions. This creates the problem for the primary caregivers of continuing to see the "whole" person. Puchalski covers the empirical research that shows what spirituality and religion can do for caregivers in this respect, and thus indirectly for their patients. In reviewing this research, she ponders some of the theological implications for how we think about these patients, and she argues for a wider scope to our conception of patients with dementia as persons, the essence of which in her view is not cognition but spiritual being.

While both Post's and Puchalski's essays argue for an approach to dementia that regards the elderly in an all-inclusive way, Roy Baumeister's essay comes from the other side. He is concerned with what happens when social inclusion is explicitly denied to human individuals. In some cases, the answer to the question Vanier noted, "Do you love me?" is a deliberate "No," which creates the condition of social exclusion. Baumeister's essay reports the results of a series of studies in psychology in which various aspects of exclusion have been investigated by means of laboratory experiments. These experiments deliberately exposed their subjects (who were not informed about it) to exclusion by others in various ways — in order to study their responses. Some readers will presumably question the ethics of this scientific methodology, as most of us did during our meeting. But Baumeister's findings turn out to be very significant. For one thing, they suggest patterns of responding to deliberate exclusion in people *without* disabilities that are very well known in people *with* disabilities. This vindicates Vanier's claim that what he has learned from his friends about the need for being accepted is a lesson about *our* humanity; it is not a lesson about *their* disability. Equally important, Baumeister's findings cast new light on the debate over the social constructionist view that disability is a social rather than a "natural" condition. His research indicates how social exclusion can become the source of withdrawal from social interaction that triggers a biological response. Furthermore, rejected people lose the ability to understand and get along with others, and this clearly indicates how social exclusion may operate as a self-fulfilling prophecy: people with disabilities may lack socially adaptive skills as an effect of being excluded rather than the other way around.

Thus, when Vanier tells us about people with disabilities suffering from being completely turned into themselves because they have been a source of shame for their parents, and hence have never learned to develop self-esteem, Baumeister's research explains how such inner psychological conditions may result from patterns of social interaction, which means that they need not be caused by the condition of disability per se. At any rate, his research vindicates Vanier's claim that the insight of psychology provides an indispensable help in enabling the "inner liberation" of people with disabilities. In his essay Vanier identifies many questions that he regards as crucial to reflecting on what he has learned from his friends. Yet all those questions push us in the same direction: to help us see how sharing his life with people with disabilities has "transformed" him. This raises the question concerning what kind of transformation is involved in the sharing of such lives, and what particulars can explain its occurrence.

That question is taken on in the papers by Kevin Reimer and Pamela Cushing, both of whom analyze the transformation process, but from quite different empirical perspectives. Looking at the process of moral transformation as a key feature of living in L'Arche, Reimer begins with a narrative that clearly exemplifies Vanier's observation that many men and women coming to that community suffer from a lack of self-esteem. Reimer's story is about a woman who explains how her experience of being raped in high school made her life miserable and very lonely before she came to L'Arche. Her story is an example of what Vanier means when he speaks of "fear of growth" due to extreme wounds of rejection. In this case it is not the condition of disability but the history of being raped — and not telling anyone — that is a source of shame (it is thus also a perfect "real-life" example of the psychological mechanism that emerges from Baumeister's research). Reimer adopts the same perspective that Vanier does when he reads the narrative as a "tangible recovery from shame" and sets out to investigate how self-conscious emotions, such as shame, can play a role in the process of moral transformation.

Pamela Cushing's essay on caregiver transformation starts with a broader picture within which rejection is part of a "persistent negative cultural outlook on disability." Where Baumeister and Reimer come from the perspective of empirical and moral psychology, Cushing's approach is that of cultural anthropology. Her project is to tap the L'Arche community as a source for imagining the lives of people with disabilities in a more positive way. Therefore, she focuses on reports in which caregivers talk about engaging in relationships with people with disabilities as an enriching experience, similar to what Vanier speaks of in his work. Cushing examines the "cultural scripts" that enable this experience. Her question concerns what cultural factors can explain how "regular people" become open to the gifts of people with disabilities. By analyzing the processes that characterize the communities of L'Arche as a cultural milieu that facilitates growth, she aims at a paradigm shift in how society might approach people with disabilities in a different way.

The countercultural force of the practices of L'Arche that is the focus of Cushing's essay highlights its particularity as a spiritual community, but this is not to deny the universal significance of these practices. The gesture of being open to the world at large is an important aspect of Vanier's work. It also resonates strongly in Xavier Le Pichon's paper. As a former resident of L'Arche, where he lived with his family (which included two disabled children), Le Pichon confirms Vanier's experience of having learned a new way of life that is quite different from what society advocates. Accordingly, he interprets the L'Arche community and its humanity as a "sign of contradiction," a phrase he borrows from Pope John Paul II. Le Pichon's paper starts with the birth of Jesus announced by Simeon as a "sign that shall be spoken against" (Luke 2: 34-35). He then explains how Jesus' way to the cross reveals the "mystery of our humanity," which he sees reflected in people with intellectual disabilities, rejected and despised by society as they usually are. Following Fr. Thomas Philippe, Le Pichon identifies infancy with its vulnerability and old age with its proximity to death as the "two golden ages of humanity." Even though our society tends to regard the dependency of human beings at these stages as atypical — an observation that Gaventa also makes — Le Pichon says that they reveal a deeper truth because they allow "the Holy Spirit to act in a very special way." It brings into the open the special gifts that accompany infancy and old age, the times of our lives that are often similar to the lives of people with developmental disabilities.

A further aspect of Le Pichon's essay, also present in Vanier's work, that I wish to focus on here is that both identify themselves as belonging to the Christian tradition, but they do not consider what L'Arche has to say to be a message particularly for Christians. Instead, they explicitly regard the gospel to be reflected in human nature. Le Pichon's essay witnesses to this characteristic in that he finds prehistoric proof for the "sign of contradiction." From the findings of paleoanthropology concerning the burial of a disabled ancestor he infers that the vulnerability at the heart of the human condition has been recognized by humanity since its origins.

It is not surprising that, in responding to the community of L'Arche, various authors have found it to be grounded in a particular kind of religious anthropology. Vanier frequently indicates his aim to be our understanding of what it means to be human, as is apparent in his recent book *Becoming Human.* This theme also runs through Post's essay, where he addresses the notion of personhood. However, Bill Gaventa addresses the subject most directly by taking on the question of what it means to be human in the same way that Vanier does, that is, by using his experience in the disability field as a source, rather than by attempting a formal philosophical or theological analysis. His experience has shown that formal questions about what it is to be human, or what it is to be disabled, often are used to provide justifications for labels distinguishing qualities and characteristics that people rely on in their specific roles as professional caregivers. However, as soon as they enter into relationships with individual people, such distinctions lose their significance. In the present case, the question of what it means to be a human person is different when it is raised about real-life people — James, John, Susan, and Diane — rather than about a class of people. Accordingly, Gaventa's main concern is asking the "right" questions. Following Vanier, Gaventa indicates that understanding the experience of people with disabilities as human experience presupposes developing communal relationships in a process of mutual growth. He then considers what the implications of that are for how we plan and organize practices of care and support. Convictions about how we are human persons should be translated in how human relationships of mutuality can be sustained.

As I have mentioned above, Vanier indicates that living with people with disabilities in L'Arche has led him to raise questions about social and political institutions in our society, and Brian Brock and Stanley Hauerwas address that theme. Brock responds to a claim that Vanier often makes: that living and working in L'Arche is not an example set by moral "heroes." The contrary view is often used to suggest that the inclusive practices of L'Arche are only possible because of its extraordinary people. Brock reconstructs this rhetorical move as a claim about supererogation, which Cushing also addresses in her essay. He locates his discussion in contemporary medical ethics as represented in *Principles of Biomedical Ethics* by Beauchamp and Childress, who suggest that accepting a child with a disability is an act of sacrificial love that exceeds the boundaries of ordinary morality. Reviewing reports in feminist studies about experiences with prenatal screening, Brock argues that the notion of sacrificial love is put before women to suggest that they do not need to accept a disabled child. This leads him to the notion of supererogation that is used to construe parenting a disabled child as an act of charity. He shows that, in advancing this notion, biomedical ethicists suggest that people fulfill an extraordinary task that exceeds the limits of moral obligation. By contrast, Brock argues that "supererogation" used in this connection excludes disabled children from the scheme of social cooperation because it implies that the only duties we have toward them are duties beyond the pale of the ordinary. He criticizes the notion of supererogation from a theological point of view. With respect to practices of prenatal screening, he claims that "after the Fall," original relationships of kinship may not be sufficient to forge the ties of moral inclusion, and, therefore, that becoming an inclusive community is a process of learning grounded in God's act of redemption.

Stanley Hauerwas's essay repeats Brock's thematic focus by looking at the implications of L'Arche as they reflect social ethics, but he does so in his own unmistakably pacifist key. Starting with Vanier's claim that sharing the life of people with disabilities has taught him that the need for peace in our world cannot be realized if not through recognizing the gifts of the "weak," Hauerwas sets out to explain his understanding of L'Arche as a peace movement. He particularly points to Vanier's insight into fear as the source of our own violence. As Vanier puts this in his essay, he has been brought closer "not only to what is most beautiful in me, but also to the world of darkness, fear and anguish within my own heart. . . . Faced with anguish I have seen violence rise up in me." Accordingly, Hauerwas interprets L'Arche as a community where people learn the habits of patience necessary to live with one another without resorting to violence. "Vanier's great gift, the gift of L'Arche, is to teach us to see pain, to enter into the pain of others, without wanting to destroy those who suffer."

Hauerwas's essay, however, operates on another level in that he wants to show how L'Arche embodies a moral epistemology. L'Arche is not an idea put into practice, he argues, just as pacifism is not a moral principle to be realized by political action. Following Wittgenstein, he explains that the order of knowledge works the other way around: "In the beginning was the deed." Therefore, Vanier and his friends did not put a politics of inclusion into practice, but they tried to live a life inspired by the way of Jesus Christ, whose peace we have received to give to one another. According to Hauerwas, L'Arche is thus more of a sign than a means for a politics of peace. This is not to deny that L'Arche has a politics, but it is of a very different nature from how politics is commonly understood in our society. Its politics of peace is a politics of time within which we take the time to do for one another what needs to be done.

Referring to a statement by Pope John Paul II, that people with disabilities are heralds of "a new world transfigured by the light of Christ," Vanier confesses to the way this has proven to be true in his own life. "People with disabilities have called forth the child in me," he says, which is a confession he makes after having explained how sharing their lives has taught him to celebrate the beauty of life. The transfiguration of becoming a child in the light of Christ means for Vanier, of course, having discovered how to be God's child. It occurs to me that John Swinton's essay carries on Vanier's witness at this point, which has nothing to do with treating people with disabilities as if they were children.

Facing a controversy about people with profound intellectual disabilities partaking of the Eucharist, Swinton raises the important question of the relationship between the sacraments and the knowledge of God. He asks whether knowing God necessarily presupposes knowing things *about* God. He generously passes by the question of whether people *without* disabilities understand the things they supposedly know about God when taking part in the Eucharist. Instead, Swinton focuses on the apophatic tradition in Christian theology. The apophatic tradition claims that theological language naming divine attributes — things we think we know about God — is inadequate because it necessarily remains on the level of intellectual representation, whereas the reality of God can only be experienced through God's presence, not through discursive language.

Swinton brings in the apophatic tradition to suggest the possibility that people with intellectual disabilities may actually "have an advantage"

13

over others when it comes to knowing and loving God, "because they don't have the distractions of the intellect to block them." Consequently, knowing God must be saved from representation through language, which Swinton tries to do by turning to the notion of practices. The point against discursive language as a means to understanding is that the issue may be more a question of "knowing how" rather than "knowing that." Turning to the tradition of liberation theology, Swinton claims that it can teach us how taking part in particular kinds of practices can teach us how to be in God's presence. It would be hard to deny that Vanier's account of celebrating life in the community of L'Arche, including people with profound disabilities, denotes a practice embodying the love of God. Elaborating on this premise, Swinton argues that taking part in such a practice is properly understood as a way of knowing God.

Finally, my own essay picks up the same theme from a different angle, which is provided by the notion of time. Our Western culture is dominated by a secular notion of time, which entails that time has no meaning other than the meaning it acquires through human plans and purposes. In view of this pervasive secular notion of time as "empty time," it cannot really be surprising that the lives of people with profound intellectual disabilities are believed to be without any meaning because they lack the subjective experience of time. They don't plan anything, and there seems to be no purpose in their lives. To counter the secular notion of empty time, I follow Jean Vanier's lead with regard to the importance of celebrating life in L'Arche. The time of celebration with food, wine, song, dance, and laughter, according to Vanier, is "the time when all can rejoice — with their disabilities and abilities — and give thanks to God for having moved us from loneliness to togetherness." Giving thanks is living in God's time, a thought that Stanley Hauerwas also expresses. Turning to Jesus' preaching about the lilies of the field, I explore a different understanding of time in the context of the divine economy. Taking the lead in reading the gospel is an essay by Søren Kierkegaard, which explains what we can learn from the lilies and the birds in terms of being content with how God has created us. Analogously, I suggest that we can learn from the disabled what it means to live our lives in God's time, namely, to be content simply with our creatureliness as human beings. That, it seems to me, is precisely what is embodied in the celebration of life in L'Arche.

The Project

Whatever it is we think there is to learn from people with disabilities — either as a society or, personally, as human individuals — there is an irreducible gap between thinking about the lives they live, even sharing their lives, on the one hand, and living with a disability, on the other. This, I believe, is the best way to explain how the essay by Christopher Newell is different from all the preceding ones in this book. Therefore, we offer it as a personal reflection regarding our project, of which Christopher was so gracious to be a part despite the considerable trouble it took him to be present at all in Trosly-Breuil.

There is a sense in which his essay makes tangible the anguish and fear of which Vanier speaks. As a member of the scientific community who suffers from a disability himself, Newell experiences the "aboutness" of scientific discourse as very alienating. Put in terms of representation, being present as someone whose identity as a person with a disability is often represented by others, which cannot but evoke the persistent demand for recognition. This is the message that people with disabilities who have invaded the domain of the sciences have expressed for the last twenty years: "Nothing about us without us." And Newell's voice is no exception to this rule. Nonetheless, I believe that his essay confirms the fundamental claim that was laid upon us — individually and as a society — by the community of L'Arche. Human vulnerability must not only be included in our scientific understanding of humanity, but it needs to be shared, and preferably not just at the fringes of our lives. Understanding the lives of people with disabilities as the sciences represent them is one thing; appreciating the presence of such people is quite another.

At this point we may consider an obvious objection to the project that resulted in this book. Doesn't the very question about what we can learn from people with disabilities — their being our "teachers," as it is put in the language of L'Arche — presuppose that they are somehow "special"? And isn't the habit of considering people with disabilities as "special" precisely what in many ways has made their lives miserable? What we hope the reader will take from these essays is that what there is to be learned from these human beings is about our own existence no less than it is about theirs. It is not their being disabled that makes them special. It is rather the experience of sharing (part of) our lives with them that makes us see things that we would otherwise easily ignore. In the final analysis, then, what we learn teaches us something about being human. Though we may learn it in engaging ourselves with people with disabilities, it is nonetheless a truth about being human per se, regardless of its state or condition.

PART II

The Call

Chapter One

What Have People with
Learning Disabilities Taught Me?

Jean Vanier

People with disabilities have taught me so much over these past forty-two years as we have lived and shared together in L'Arche as friends and companions, as brothers and sisters, as people brought together by God. In fact, they have not only taught me; they have *transformed* me and brought me into a new and deeper vision of humanity.

They are helping me discover who I am, what my deepest needs are, and what it means to be human. They have led me into a new and meaningful way of life quite different from what society advocates. They have revealed to me the need for community in our societies and that those who are weak and vulnerable have something important to bring to our world today.

Before l'Arche, I was searching — not quite knowing what I was searching for. I had developed my capacities as a naval officer and had learned to be disciplined and efficient. I also studied and taught philosophy. Like everyone else, I wanted to do well and be appreciated by my superiors. My belief in Jesus and my desire to know and live the gospel message were important to me, but I had not yet found my "earth," my anchor, my resting place. I am profoundly grateful to people with learning disabilities because with them I have found this "earth": I have a found a unity between my life and my faith, between what is interior and exterior, between what I think, feel, and understand and what I do.

This may give the impression that the founding of l'Arche was simply a process of self-searching and only for self-fulfillment. This is, of course, partly true. However, I fundamentally believe that l'Arche began as a response to a cry that I first heard when I visited an institution for thirty men with learning disabilities where Fr. Thomas Philippe, a friend, was chaplain. This cry, "Do you love me? Am I important? Will you be my friend?" was expressed or written on the faces of those men and of many others in different institutions and of those living in painful situations. I wanted to create a place where they could find inner freedom, develop their personhood and abilities, and be fulfilled, where they could let their deepest desires rise up and find a new meaning for their lives.

Many of those who came to l'Arche were in deep need. They carried within their hearts the wounds of rejection. They suffered from a lack of self-esteem and from major physical and psychological difficulties. Some were prone to violence or had self-destructive attitudes and a fear of growth. It was clear to me that in order to be a place of growth, healing, and inner liberation, L'Arche needed the help of good professionals. Thanks to many psychiatrists and other professionals, I am learning an inner wisdom of bringing together the resources of human sciences (psychology), ethics, spirituality, and religion. I am learning the necessity of creating a milieu of life where people can find inner healing and which has clear structures integrated into the social, political, and health systems in a country. I am learning about the need for prayer and spirituality, not only for people with learning difficulties but for everybody. I am discovering more fully the place of church and of a religious affiliation. I am discovering a lot about the human person and the purpose of education: to bring people not just to greater autonomy and independence but also to greater maturity. Let me point out just a few things I have seen and experienced during these forty-two years.

1. Each person, whatever his or her abilities or disabilities, needs to be nurtured in love. The desire to be loved as a person, as someone unique, is at the source of the person's development and at the source of all self-esteem. When this need is not fulfilled, a deep wound is implanted in the heart. Many people with disabilities have been regarded by their parents as a disappointment and a source of shame. This profoundly wounds children. In order to grow to greater fulfillment, these children need a place of belonging where they feel loved and respected.

2. The fear in couples of giving birth to a child with a disability is imprinted in the culture of every society. They are often seen as "subhuman," and they are rejected — or put aside in some way. Many are

aborted if the existence of an abnormality is detected in the mother's womb. Many are put away in large institutions. Throughout the world, hundreds and hundreds of institutions exist where people with learning disabilities live in inhuman conditions.

3. The values many modern societies hold are independence, individualism, and success for every citizen. More traditional societies are respectful of the old and the sick, but even they are often unable to see people with learning disabilities as important. In richer societies, the weak are seen as an economic and human liability. And so people with learning disabilities are pushed to the margins of society.

4. Many people with learning disabilities need help from professionals in order to overcome physical and psychological difficulties, to grow to greater autonomy, and to develop their capacities in various fields. But, above all, they are yearning for meaningful, authentic, respectful, and committed relationships. Their cry for love flows also from their deep loneliness and their lack of self-esteem. They have called me to listen and to respond to their cry with competence, to welcome their vulnerability with tenderness, and then to be in communion with them. As we respond to this fundamental cry for friendship, they begin to transform and to heal us. We can either hide our vulnerability behind a strong, protective ego, or else we can discover that our vulnerability is a source of communion and unity. We do not need to control or have power over them. We can be in communion with one another, offering to each other our mutual need for one another. In this way they have awoken in me what is deepest and most precious: a desire to give life to others and to receive life from them through a communion of hearts.

In 1978 we welcomed Eric into one of our homes here in Trosly. He was sixteen and had spent twelve of those sixteen years in the children's ward of a psychiatric hospital. Eric had severe learning disabilities, but was also blind and deaf and unable to walk by himself. I don't think I have ever seen a young person filled with so much anguish. He just wanted to die. What meaning could life have for him? Our aim in L'Arche is to transform the broken self-image of someone like Eric into a positive self-image, the wish to die into a desire to live. When I left the leadership of the community, I spent a year in Eric's home for ten people with severe disabilities. His utter littleness and poverty, the moments of gentle trust, awoke in me a deep feeling of compassion. In the morning when we would bathe him in the warm water, his whole body would relax and manifest that he was happy. As the months went by, he became more and more peaceful. Eric taught me so much about being attentive to wounded, vulnerable persons: how to interpret their body language and live a communion of hearts with them.

People like Eric have led me into the need for community and for a simple lifestyle where the essential is to care for one another, to celebrate life, to be open, and to grow more loving and understanding toward neighbors and friends, a lifestyle where we are no longer each for ourselves alone, but together we are a sign of a new way of life, where the weak and the vulnerable and the marginalized have their place.

John Paul II said something to this effect in a document he wrote in 2004 for a symposium on the "Dignity and Rights of Disabled People":

> It is said, justifiably so, that disabled people are humanity's privileged witnesses. They can teach everyone about the love that saves us; they can become heralds of a new world, no longer dominated by force, violence and aggression, but by love, solidarity and acceptance, a new world transfigured by the light of Christ, the Son of God who became incarnate, who was crucified and rose for us.

Since people with learning disabilities are limited in their capacity to rationalize and form ideas, and their verbal language is limited, they tend to communicate more through their bodily gestures and simple words of love, or of anger. Through them I have discovered the importance of work and interesting activities for their personal development, but their desire to celebrate life and have fun are even more important because they are a sign of mutual belonging. In this way they call us all to celebrations that bring people together with all that is beautiful: food, wine, song, dance, laughter, dress, decoration. It is a time when all can rejoice — with their abilities and disabilities — and give thanks to God for having moved us all from loneliness to togetherness. The child within my own self has learned to laugh and celebrate and give thanks for all that bonds us together. People with disabilities have called forth the child in me. They have taught us all in L'Arche how to rest in love and mutual caring, how to celebrate life and also celebrate death, to speak about death, to accompany people who are dying. Death is a part of life: it is not something to be terrified about, but rather is the final passage into a new life.

As those who are weak and vulnerable have called forth in me the wisdom of love, they have also made me more vulnerable. I have been brought closer not only to what is most beautiful in me, but also to the world of darkness, fear, and anguish within my own heart, to all my own difficulties in relationships, and to my need to prove myself. Faced with their anguish, I have seen violence rise up in me. But since I live in community and have the support of my brothers and sisters in the community, this violence is contained. It is only when we touch the powers of destruction within us and begin to accept that they are there, but do not let ourselves be controlled or governed by them, that we can truly understand and accept others in their anguish — and then help them to grow.

Martin Luther King said that people cannot stop despising others — as well as other groups of people — unless they begin to accept what is despicable in themselves. What is it that we all despise in ourselves? Isn't it our radical poverty, our utter helplessness in many situations, our need of others, our mortality, and our capacity to hurt others? We did not ask to be born. We do not know when or how we will die. We do not possess life. We received it. I have discovered that this helplessness makes me turn more to God and to my brothers and sisters in community. I cannot say that I have accepted all that is despicable in me, but I am more aware of my need for transformation.

I can also say that living with those who have known rejection and have been despised has opened up my heart to the pain of all those throughout the world who are "different," who have experienced rejection and hatred because of a disability or not. They, too, need love so that they no longer live closed up in fear but open up in trust. I have come to the realization that peace cannot come to our societies and our world unless those who are rich and powerful accept loss and a certain helplessness in order to enter into authentic relationships with those who are weak, vulnerable, and powerless, and unless the latter rise up from their depression, aggression, and anger and find trust in themselves and in others. This can only come about if we rediscover new ways for the weak and the strong, the rich and the poor, to meet each other and to discover their common humanity.

In this way, the cry of the weak and the vulnerable can bring together people of different religious traditions. They can become a source of unity. After participating in an interreligious pilgrimage with people with learning disabilities in Bangladesh, the Taizé Brothers wrote the following:

We discover more and more that those who are rejected by society because of their weakness and their apparent uselessness are in fact a presence of God. If we welcome them, they lead us progressively out of a world of competition and the need to do great things, towards a world of communion of hearts, a life that is simple and joyful, where we do small things with love. The challenge today in our country urges us on to show that the service of our weak and vulnerable brothers and sisters means opening a way of peace and unity: welcoming each other in the rich diversity of religions and cultures, serving the poor together, preparing a future of peace.

People with learning disabilities are leading me more fully into an understanding of the gospel message and of the life of Jesus. Jesus' life and message are for all, but in a special way for those who have been cast aside. To enter into the kingdom of God we need to become like little children. Saint Paul tells us that God has chosen the weak and foolish in the eyes of the world and that they are necessary — indeed, indispensable — for the church, which is the body of Christ. So many of us intellectualize this message of Jesus and remain inside our own heads. People with disabilities have helped me to realize that it is a message of the heart, a message of love and of humility adapted to those who cry out, "Do you love me?" and who are open to a personal relationship with God. This cry for relationship from people who are weak and vulnerable has helped me to live closer to Jesus, the Word who became flesh, vulnerable and little, the one who begs each one of us to receive him into our hearts so that we may receive others into our hearts.

PART III

Responses from the Sciences

Chapter Two

Drawing Closer: Preserving Love in the Face of "Hypercognitive" Values

STEPHEN G. POST

Introduction

An adequate ethical theory or moral life requires us to include everyone within the moral domain of care and respect. This universalism asserts that all human lives have equal moral standing with the exception of those who are dead by brain-death criteria. There is a troubling tendency, however, to exclude human beings from moral concern while they are still among the living. This occurs most frequently when we differentiate "them" from "us," depersonalizing and dehumanizing others for reasons of race, class, gender, age, culture, or cognitive disabilities, including forgetfulness. Under such circumstances of exclusion, we easily set aside the principle of the inviolability of the other, and we ignore the requirement of meeting the other's basic human needs. The core concern of ethics, then, is the deep affirmation of a common humanity. There is no reason to exclude anyone from that affirmation based on the mere fact that that person has become more deeply forgetful than the rest of us, or never developed the normal range of cognitive abilities.

Yet philosophers with hypercognitive values (Post 1995, 32) often diminish the moral status of the cognitively impaired. The cognitively limited fall outside of the protective range of "do no harm," they argue,

---

I wish to acknowledge the John Templeton Foundation, the Institute for Research on Unlimited Love, Tom Kitwood, and Jean Vanier for inspiring this essay.

though their deaths should be painless, of course. Infanticide is acceptable because infants are not rational moral agents, and senicide is a fitting end for the forgetful (Singer 1997, 93).

The alternative response to the cognitively imperiled is to enlarge our sense of human worth by de-emphasizing the moral significance of rationality, the efficient use of time and energy, the ability to control distracting impulses, thrift, economic success, self-reliance, language advantage, and the like. We make too much of these things. The great Stoic philosophers achieved much for universal human moral standing by emphasizing the spark of reason *(logos)* in us all. However, this is an arrogant view in the sense that it makes the worth of a human being entirely dependent on rationality, and then gives too much power to the reasonable. Reinhold Niebuhr, taking what he considered to be the Christian view, concluded that "since the divine principle is reason, the logic of Stoicism tends to include only the intelligent in the divine community. An aristocratic condescension, therefore, corrupts Stoic universalism" (Niebuhr 1956, 53).

Hypercognitive values are especially in need of correction when it comes to those imperiled persons in whom cognitive development is hampered, or in whom older age brings with it the onset of dementia. The abstract nature of hypercognitive values is perhaps their undoing, for in drawing closer to people with cognitive disabilities, we often are inspired by their ability to give and respond to love; and we discover that love, rather than cognitive dexterity, is the most fundamental aspect of humanness and the ultimate basis for moral status. Even those who are severely disabled maintain this humanness at some level of residual capacity.

Drawing Closer: The Discovery and Power of Love

Hypercognitivism is a form of bias against those with cognitive disabilities that interferes with our sense of a shared or common humanity. But lived experience with such people can overcome this bias when we are inspired by their abilities, and we begin to see how much they can teach us. Let me provide an example of a transformative experience that I had some years ago.

I met Mr. G. in 1988 in a nursing home in Chardon, Ohio. He taught me that love is the ultimate reality that ties our lives together. I read a brief biographical sketch about his life, and then sat down to talk with him. I asked him how his sons were doing. Although he could not understand or respond, he placed a twig in my hands and gave me a huge warm smile. I thanked him and then gave it back. I asked the nurse to tell me about the twig. She said that when Mr. G. was a little boy growing up on an Ohio farm, he loved his father very much. Every morning his father gave the boy the chore of bringing in kindling for the fireplace. Mr. G. had retreated back in time to his boyhood, to a period of fatherly love that provided an emotional safe haven. The twig was a profound symbol of who he was and who he is. Mr. G. later picked up an old ragged puppet doll from the floor and handed it to a woman who was crying, at which point she, too, smiled, for it belonged to her.

I learned from Mr. G. a certain freedom from the pressure of having to project and implement plans for the future, and from the need to control the future or the present. He showed me that it is possible to give love without the executive cognitive function that restricts us to the social laws of reciprocal calculation or reputational gain. Mr. G. demonstrated that love remains powerful even in the midst of cognitive decline. I walked away inspired to tend to the reality of love in all the people I might encounter that day, and determined to be a little more like Mr. G.

Jean Vanier provided me with two stories about the power of love in the lives of people with cognitive disabilities, and about the transformations that those around them sometimes undergo.

> The wife of a friend, who was a wealthy businessman, developed Alzheimer's disease. He decided not to put her in an institution but to care for her at home. He feeds her, gives her a bath, and looks after all her everyday needs. Not long ago he confided to me: "I am becoming more human." His heart has been awoken. His grandson told a friend of mine: "Yes, my grandfather has changed totally. He used to be so rigid and difficult. We always had to watch how we behaved at meals. Now, during the meals, his wife says all kinds of funny things that don't make much sense. And Grandpa is so gentle and kind with her and with us all."

And another story:

> Just recently the mother of Pauline came to visit her daughter, a nineteen-year-old assistant living and working in one of our homes. Pauline has been in the home only four months. Her mother told me how her daughter has changed and been transformed. Before coming here she was unable to make choices, didn't know who she was nor

[what she] wanted for the future. Now she has discovered that she is giving life to the people with disabilities around her. She is loved by them and new energies of caring and of communion are flowing from her. People with disabilities have awoken her heart and what is deepest within her: her capacity to give life and to bring joy and hope to others.

These are stories about people drawing closer to those with cognitive disabilities and, in the process, being reawakened to a life of greater love.

What can we learn from people with disabilities? First, we can learn that gift-love will often be the capacity that remains behind after cognition has faded. Second, we can go to that emotional ground with people with disabilities and discover what is most central to the human essence.

Drawing Closer: Two Exemplars

For me, the two most inspiring people in the field of ethics, spirituality, and care for persons with cognitive disabilities have been Jean Vanier and the late Tom Kitwood, who was director of the Dementia Institute at the University of Bradford in England. Vanier, a Canadian, is a Catholic whose work is faith-based; Kitwood, who won a parliamentary award in England for his work, was a Methodist minister before turning to his mission on behalf of the most profoundly forgetful. Although they were contemporaries and were both known internationally, they never knew of each other's work.

I find it intriguing that both Vanier and Kitwood argue forcefully that the credible basis for quality of life and moral status in the lives of people with cognitive disabilities derives from love. In his book *Becoming Human*, Vanier includes revelation of worth or value as the first feature of love in the context of persons with cognitive disabilities: "To reveal someone's beauty is to reveal their value by giving them time, attention, and tenderness" (Vanier 1998, 22). Understanding, communication, and the celebration of the other's life in a personal manner convey a liberating and an empowering sense of worth. In *Dementia Reconsidered: The Person Comes First* (1997), Tom Kitwood's classic work, his definition of love within the context of care for those with dementia includes comfort in the original sense of tenderness, closeness, the calming of anxiety, and bonding. Kitwood defines the main psychological needs of persons with dementia in terms of care or love. He draws on the narratives of caregivers to assert that persons with dementia want love, "a generous, forgiving and unconditional acceptance, a wholehearted emotional giving, without any expectation of direct reward." The first component of love is giving comfort, which includes tenderness, calming of anxiety, and bolstering feelings of security based on affective closeness. It is especially important for the person with dementia who retains a sense of his or her lost capacities. Attachment, the second component of love, includes the formation of specific bonds that enhance a feeling of security. Inclusion in social experiences, occupation in activities that draw on a person's abilities and powers, and, finally, identity are important components of love.

Vanier and Kitwood both argue that the person with cognitive disabilities will respond better to a caregiver whose affect is affirming in tone, and that people with disabilities themselves are capable of being the instruments of love. I find in Vanier and Kitwood a common underlying definition of love that is grounded in emotional affirmation and undistracted presence. When the happiness and security of the person with cognitive disabilities comes to mean as much to us as our own happiness and security, we love that person. That love is the only real hope for the person, and through that transforming experience we come to realize that it is the only real hope for ourselves. Neither Vanier nor Kitwood emphasizes self-sacrifice; rather, both focus on the fulfillment that a life of love for people with cognitive disabilities affords us as agents. Therefore, love is a resurrection-of-a-sort for the disabled person, and it is equally so for us the caregivers.

Enhancing the Quality of Life Through Love

Both Vanier and Kitwood emphasize that people with cognitive disabilities do give love back, so this is not a unilateral phenomenon. Both the disabled person and the one caring for that person give love. In this sense, the dynamic of mutual love enhances both parties to the relationship. But it must be said that the caregiver has a special responsibility to use love to enhance the life of the disabled individual.

Love elicits a sense of joy in the receiver, who feels inwardly "a home in which it is safe." Those who receive this affective affirmation will sense a freedom from anxiety — that is, a certain safe haven in love where the stress of devaluation and isolation is removed. Human beings need such love, both emotionally and physiologically, and this is what we learn from those with cognitive disabilities. People tend to remember well over the years those from whom they receive warm, generous love; conversely, people also remember those who have shamed and humiliated them. The opposite of love can be observed in episodes of malignant social psychology, which include intimidation, stigmatization, invalidation, objectification, mockery, and disparagement.

The first principle of love for persons with cognitive disability is to reveal to them their value by providing attention, concern, and tenderness. Any experienced caregiver knows that the person with dementia, however advanced, will usually respond better to someone whose affect is affirming in tone. Emotional, relational, aesthetic, and spiritual forms of well-being are possible to varying degrees in people with cognitive deficits. There is a "culture of dementia" that is useful in appreciating emotional and relational aspects of quality of life. There are indicators of well-being in people with severe dementia: the assertion of will or desire, usually in the form of dissent despite various coaxings; the ability to express a range of emotions; initiation of social contact (for instance, a person with dementia has a small toy dog that he treasures and places in front of another person with dementia to attract attention); affectionate warmth (for instance, a woman wanders back and forth in the facility without much socializing, but when people say hello to her she gives them a kiss on the cheek and continues her wandering) (Kitwood 1997).

The aesthetic well-being available to people with Alzheimer's disease (AD) is obvious to anyone who has watched therapy sessions using art or music. In some cases, a person with advanced AD may still draw the same valued symbol, as though a sense of self can be retained through art (Firlik 1991). Some years ago I was involved in the development of *Memories in the Making,* a nationwide program that explores whether people with dementia can reveal themselves through art. Many artists from around the United States now volunteer to lead these programs in most major cities and towns. What we have discovered is that even in the most advanced stages of the disease, individuals will express remnants of self-identity. They may not be able to communicate by speech or proceed from point A to point B over time; indeed, most are living in the pure present, and they seem to be utterly "gone." But we need to be careful about such assumptions, and we need to allow these people opportunities to express their self-identity through the re-creation of a symbol.

In October 2006, the *Columbia Daily Tribune* (Missouri) ran an article that noted my interest in this project over the years. I told the reporter of a man with AD who clung to his cowboy hat until the very end of his life, even bathing and sleeping with it. It turned out that he had worked in the steel factories and dressed "country and western." He knew his identity was somehow connected with that cowboy hat. The newspaper article ends with a comment from Debra Brook, the local director of the Alzheimer's Association in Columbia, who told of one elderly man with AD who, barely able to communicate, did not recognize his daughter any longer. "When the man joined the Memories in the Making program," Ms. Brook said, "he worked for weeks drawing a series of horizontal and diagonal lines on paper. When asked what he was drawing, he said, 'Directions to my daughter's house.'" Despite his decline, this man was still expressing love for his daughter through creativity.

Love, Inclusion, and a Common Humanity

We easily demean those whose memory has dissipated by treating them with indifference or even cruelty. This indifference is seen when we neglect to speak with persons with dementia, make eye contact with them, or call them by name, expecting a response. Whether it is the waiter in a restaurant or the doctor in the clinic, there is a tendency to speak about or around someone with dementia, rather than with them. We act as if they aren't there. Once — less than seven decades ago — the step between psychological and physical elimination proved notoriously short. As part of the Nazi extermination program, known as T-4, persons with dementia, selected for hypothermia experiments, were taken out of German mental asylums and left to freeze in the cold overnight air. Memory is a form of power. We sometimes mock and ignore those who have lost such power, sending the message that their very existence rests on a mistake (Post 2000).

It is remarkable that some people seem to want to do the best they can for the deeply forgetful — even Professor Peter Singer. Ordinary people disagree with the occasional philosopher who asserts in an essay that those who have lost temporal glue, who are more or less consigned to the pure present, should be painlessly eliminated because they no longer have moral standing.

I reject all attempts to pick out one property as the basis for moral consideration, for this monism is inevitably arbitrary and invites exclusion. Some philosophers pick the property of rationality as that one property. They generally define rationality procedurally, as an ability to do cer-

33

tain things, such as act consistently based on clear thinking, arrive at decisions by deliberation, envision a future for oneself, and so forth. In fact, however, rather few of us go through life with consistent rationality (Zagzebski 2001). We act on emotion, intuition, impulse, and the like. We go through periods of considerable irrationality due to our variations in mood. Young children have limited reasoning capacities, but we do not devalue them. Moreover, rationality as a decisional capacity is not morally important. It is rationality as a source of self-identity that matters, that is, *who* we are rather than *how* we proceed.

Our task as moral agents is to remind persons with dementia of their continuing self-identity. We must serve as a prosthesis that fills in the gaps and expects that now and again the cues we provide will connect with the person and perhaps even elicit a surprising verbal or affective response. In other words, our task is to preserve identity. It is for this reason that many nursing homes will post biographical sketches on the doors of residents, or family members will remind a loved one of events and people who have been meaningful along life's journey. We must see the glass of self-identity as half-full rather than half-empty, and we must understand that metaphors such as "gone" or "husk" are dehumanizing and empirically suspect.

It is residual self-consciousness that we must respect and, when possible, enhance through relational stimulation. This is why, for example, it is important to address every person with AD by name. Bend down, make eye contact, and call the person by name as if expecting an answer, even if one does not come. This action is more than symbolic: it is a way of affirming residual self-consciousness, and this affirmation is morally crucial.

Conclusions

Some while ago, I received the following e-mail written by a daughter soon after her father had died:

> Hello Dear Friends:
>
> As many of you know, my father has been suffering from Alzheimer's disease for the past 4.5 years. It has been a long and often very hard road for him, for my mom, and for me too. However, as of 7 p.m. last night, my father no longer has to struggle with the disease that robbed him of every part of his being, except one. He never once stopped recognizing my mom and never, ever stopped reaching out to her and want-

ing to give her a kiss. No matter how many parts of his personality were lost, no matter how many hospital visits full of needles and catheters, no matter how many diapers, he always retained his kind, gentle sweetness and his European manners as a gentleman. In the end, things went very quickly for him. He simply closed his eyes and closed his mouth, indicating no more food or water.

The father described above was in the advanced and therefore terminal stage of AD, marked by some combination of the inabilities to communicate by speech, recognize loved ones, maintain bowel and/or bladder control, walk without assistance, and swallow without assistance. Yet, throughout all that, he seems to have benefited greatly from the giving and receiving of love, consistent with the relational context that he found meaningful over his life course. There was no assertion of a radical disconnection between the "then" intact self and the "now" demented self; instead, the subtle expressions of continuity in subjective experience and lingering self-identity were honored.

Saint Paul, in the book of 1 Corinthians, tells us to speak in the spirit of love, and that without this spirit our words are unbecoming: *"Though I speak with the tongues of mortals and of angels, but have not love, I am as a sounding gong or a clanging cymbal"* (1 Cor. 13:1). It is the affective tone of our words, our facial expressions, and our actions that draw people with cognitive disabilities into the light of love. And we discover in this exchange that such people are as able as we are when it comes to the expression of a generous heart. Parents of children with Down syndrome so often say that their children have a "happy" countenance, and this may well be related to their generosity. It is in the meek that God has perhaps chosen to reveal a love that we are too busy and hypercognitive to appreciate as the foundation of our own very lives. There is a saying in the constitutions of the Society of the Holy Child Jesus: "God has chosen to need men and women in every age to reveal his love, to make known the reality of the incarnation."

References

Firlik, A. D. 1991. Margo's logo. *Journal of the American Medical Association* 265: 201.

Kitwood, T. 1997. *Dementia reconsidered: The person comes first.* Philadelphia: Open University Press.

Niebuhr, Reinhold. 1956. *An interpretation of Christian ethics.* New York: Meridian.

Post, S. G. 1995. *The moral challenge of Alzheimer disease.* 1st ed. Baltimore: The Johns Hopkins University Press.

Post, S. G. 2000. *The moral challenge of Alzheimer disease: Ethical issues from diagnosis to dying.* 2nd ed. Baltimore: The Johns Hopkins University Press.

Singer, P. 1993. *Practical ethics.* Cambridge: Cambridge University Press.

Vanier, J. 1998. *Becoming human.* Mahwah, NJ: Paulist Press.

Zagzebski, L. 2001. The uniqueness of persons. *Journal of Religious Ethics* 29 (3): 401-23.

Chapter Three

Dementia: A Spiritual Journey
for the Patient and the Caregivers

CHRISTINA M. PUCHALSKI

Introduction

"Hello, Mom, how are you?"

"Not so good," she answered. "I don't know who all these strangers are in my home. The man is very nice, though. Who are you?"

Those words went searing through my heart. This was what I had dreaded all these years since my mother was diagnosed with dementia. I knew there were no people in her home, and the person who was there — my father, her husband — was now just a nice man. I felt so sad for my mother. Her voice quivered with an uncertain anxiety. Strangers were never people my mother felt comfortable with, and now her house was filled with them. I wanted desperately to take her confusion away, but how could I? I was one of those strangers.

Where were the memories? The times we sat and laughed on the beach, the times she held me in my own grief, or all those conversations we had about life and its ups and downs. She had been a strong woman: she had escaped from Poland during World War II and had survived suffering and horrendous loss. During her adulthood she experienced some depression, never quite being able to put the wartime pains behind her. But she was able to reach out to others with tremendous compassion and love. She was also a dignified woman who did not readily make friends or share her feelings openly. However, she respected all people and treated everyone with the utmost dignity and respect. I remember the tears she shed when she saw a person or an animal suffer. Many times she defended an elderly person or a child who was being harshly treated by someone. She stood for justice for all, especially for the disenfranchised or vulnerable.

My mother's private faith in God had sustained her during the difficult times and given her the resilience she needed to survive the vicissitudes of life. She had been highly independent all her life; now she was this frail and vulnerable person. Her independence was threatened each time my father or I changed her Depends and helped her with her activities of daily living. How many times did she tell me that she never wanted to face the end of her life in this kind of condition?

Where is my mother's dignity today? What gives her life meaning? Is there value to her life even in the face of a complete loss of memory of who she was and what she did? And for my father and me, when so much of our meaning has stemmed in part from our connection to her, where is that meaning now? Where is the relationship?

In aging — and particularly in dementia — we let go of all the externals of our lives. This may be the holiest of phases of our spiritual journeys, a time of progressive detachment from objects, accomplishments, health, and all the externals to which we so readily attach importance and meaning. Aging and dementia force us into an inward journey toward emptiness, where we face who we are without the images we have clung to all our lives. And for the caregivers of people with dementia, it may be a profound challenge in spiritual formation. Not only are caregivers forced to reevaluate the relationship with their loved one, but they are forced to see in themselves the impermanence of life, health, and earthly existence in general.

Dementia: A Progressive Decline?

Dementia is a challenging illness in that people lose their ability to think clearly, their memories fail, and over time they lose the ability to care for themselves. Personality changes and difficulty with abstract thinking and orientation are also primary symptoms. The chief defining characteristics of one type of dementia, Alzheimer's disease, are senile plaques of amyloid proteins that are found between nerve cells in the brain, and this inhibits message transmission between brain cells. It's these protein fibers that are thought to cluster in brain cell nuclei and gradually obliterate the memory. Other types of dementia include vascular (stroke-related) and dementia associated with illnesses such as alcoholism, Parkinson's disease, and others. Typical symptoms include loss of cognitive functioning, loss of judgment, and personality changes. In dementia people lose not only memory and language; they also lose their personal identity as they have defined themselves all their lives.

Sutcliff (2001) defines dementia as the progression in which the "brain goes through a long process of failure, beginning with a slight loss of memory and progressing to a total inability to cope with any aspect of life." In a society that equates intelligence, rational thought, and high functioning with essential aspects of a valuable life, a person with dementia is seen as less valuable, less of a human being, because of his or her disabilities. I have heard people with dementia described in a variety of ways: "There's no one at home." "She's a living vegetable." "He's no longer a person." People find it challenging to relate to people in a way that is nonlinear, nonrational, and nonverbal. Thus the person with dementia is further isolated from others. But dementia is not a loss of personhood; rather, it is a process of progressive decline of people's mental function.

Dementia, therefore, poses challenges for both patients and caregivers. Some might argue that spiritual care might be difficult to give to people with advanced dementia because of patients' inability to fully interact with their caregivers. I would suggest that this is false. Data certainly supports the role of spirituality in the lives of caregivers of patients with dementia, and ethical principles support spiritual care for patients with dementia. Regardless of mental functioning, every human being is a person who has the inherent right to be treated with love, dignity, and respect.

Data Supporting Spirituality in Patients and Caregivers with Dementia

Research has been done on people with dementia in nursing care and pastoral care, but only as related to the spiritual needs of the elderly whose cognitive abilities are only minimally impaired — that is, in the very early stages of dementia. Pastoral care and nursing literature deal with the issue of dementia primarily from behavioral or psychological perspectives, focusing extensively on the spiritual needs of the *caregiver*. This is probably due to a lack of a theoretical framework, which could be used to understand what is happening spiritually to the patient with dementia.

In the studies looking at caregivers, many studies have noted that spiritual beliefs help family caregivers with the stresses of caring for people with dementia. The key stressors in families of those who have dementia may have to do with uncertainty. Blank (1999) shows that the stressors identified by caregivers include coping with added responsibilities, the fear of being alone, guilt, and limited knowledge regarding the patient's situation. Two of these, guilt and dealing with uncertainty, have to do with spiritual issues. Uncertainty is a key stressor in the lives of caregivers of patients with dementia. Each person with dementia has his or her own way of exhibiting symptoms and own rate of decline. It is very hard to predict exact prognoses and outcomes. There is a waxing and waning that patients — and hence caregivers — experience. There is little known as to what extent the person with dementia understands and feels. Thus, every interaction with a loved one with dementia can provoke uncertainty and hence some anxiety and pain.

Folkman and colleagues (1994) show that increased stress motivated the engagement of religious coping in caregivers (see also Kaye and Robinson 1994). Cupertino shows that caregivers who felt closer to God, prayed frequently, and believed religion to be important were better able to cope and also experienced less stress with the caregiving demands. They felt more useful, found new meaning in life, experienced strengthened relationships, and were more able to appreciate life (Cupertino et al. 1998). Jivanjee (1994), using a naturalistic methodology, did a descriptive study of caregivers of patients with Alzheimer's disease. Spiritual support was consistently mentioned by all but two of the eighteen participants in the study as being central to their sense of well-being and giving them the strength to cope with the demands of caregiving.

Ellison and Levin (1998) postulate that religion and spirituality may be a resource in coping with stressful events. Caregivers who were able to find positive religious values in negative situations or found religious purpose in stress were better able to cope. Those who saw illness as a punishment from God or saw God as apathetic or unfair did worse (Mickley et al. 1998). Religion and spirituality may help in coping because they alter the primary appraisal that reframes the meaning or explanation of the crisis, improve a sense of secondary control because the family feels a greater power is in control, and modify an individual's identity so that the problem is less stressful and less threatening, and finally help people cope with the emotions arising from the crisis. Baines (1984) demonstrated that caregiving burdens can be relieved by increasing one's spiritual perspective to reframe the experience of grief and loss. I know from my own experience of watching my father deal with the stress of the day-to-day total care of my mother that it is his faith in God and complete surrender to God's will that gives him not only strength but meaning and purpose in everything he does for and with my mother.

Kaye and Robinson (1994) found in their study of those giving care to people with Alzheimer's disease that the well-being of female caregivers is affected by confronting end-of-life issues. Confronting issues of mortality and loss may enhance the importance of spirituality in the individual's life (Reed 1994). Other researchers suggest that caregiving results in increased feelings of depression and need for social support (Lindgren 1993; Kuhlman et al. 1994). Spirituality was shown to improve depression and enhance social support among caregiving wives. Robinson and Kaye (1994) further described spiritual practices that the caregivers used, which included:

- Talking with friends and family about spiritual matters
- Reading spiritually related material
- Engaging in private prayer
- Seeking spiritual guidance

Caregivers further described spirituality as important in everyday life, forgiveness as an important part of spirituality, and feeling close to God or a higher power in prayer, worship, and important moments in life.

Chang and colleagues (1998), in a study examining the factors that influence and are influenced by religious/spiritual coping among those providing care for disabled adults, show that religious/spiritual coping reduces symptoms of depression and role submersion. This effect is due to higher relationship quality. The authors hypothesize that religion and spirituality may play a role in sustaining human relationships that are often strained by the necessities of providing care for others. This study speaks to the relational aspects of spirituality.

Living with Uncertainty Can Contribute to Stress in the Lives of Patients and Caregivers

In one study of those giving care to patients with HIV, living in the present moment became the "anchor in the lives of many caregivers as they struggled with the uncertain future and focused on the present" (Brown and Powell-Cope 1991). The concept of living in the present moment is found in religious traditions and in spiritual programs such as the twelve-step program (Alcoholics Anonymous 1976). A focus group analysis of family members of patients on peritoneal and hemodialysis found that uncertainty related to prognosis and potential loss was the highest source of stress for the family members (Ferrans and Powers 1993). Coping strategies included:

- Living each day as it comes
- Finding positive meaning
- Hoping for a good outcome
- Drawing support from their faith in God

Other studies have looked at the role of religion and/or spirituality as helping with coping. Segall and Wykle (1989), in their study of African-American family members of patients with dementia, found religion to be the major form of coping. Richardson and Sistler (1999), in their study of African-American caregivers of patients with dementia, also found religion to be a major coping strategy, including church attendance, prayer, belief in God, Bible study, prayer meetings, and social support.

Pierce (2001) examined caring and expressions of spirituality in African-American family caregivers of stroke victims. Caring was described as:

- A filial ethereal value
- Self-contemplation
- Motivation for philosophical introspection
- Filial piety
- Living in the moment and hoping for the future
- Purpose
- Motivation that came from the approval by care recipients
- Christian piety

The commitment to care for a person who had suffered a stroke was thus based on the values of commitment, love and affection, and on the spiritual values of connection, religious values, and meaning and purpose. Jones and her colleagues (2002), in their study of female Asian-American caregivers of elderly parents, found that the women approached their caregiving challenges with devout commitment to filial responsibility. They described being "grateful for the love and care their parents gave them and wanting to give back to their parents." Love and respect were a major part of the commitment. The authors show how connection with inner strength and with their life purpose might help in coping with caregiving demands. Women identified inner strength as a primary personal resource that enabled them to deal with the demands of caregiving. Moloney (1995) analyzed older women's handling of difficult situations and found that connecting with their inner selves empowered women to integrate into the caregiving experience, to derive meaning from the experience, and to grow personally. These studies reflect the importance of cultural, religious, and spiritual values in how caregivers come to understand their roles and how they cope with stress.

Forbes (1994) examined the relationship between caregivers' and patients' concepts of spirituality measured as spiritual well-being. She found a strong correlation between a caregiver's spiritual well-being and the caregiver's perception of the patient's spiritual well-being: this suggested that the effect of the relationship of patient to caregiver is influential in the caregiver's spiritual well-being. Forbes suggests that highly significant correlations between the spiritual well-being of the caregiver and that of the patient imply that a spiritual bonding occurs. She also notes that prayer is a significant coping mechanism for caregivers. This is critical when thinking about ways to relate to people with dementia. While a verbal or intellectual connection may not be possible, a spiritual connection may be primary and may provide great comfort to both parties.

Spiritual Care for Patients with Dementia

Recent work in the United States has included the development of courses in medical schools on spirituality and health, where spirituality is defined broadly as "that which gives ultimate meaning to a person's life and which can be expressed through religious beliefs and practices but also through other types of beliefs and practices including relationships, arts and humanities" (AAMC 1994). Integral to these courses is the ethical foundation that every person has value regardless of disability. An interdisciplinary model of spiritual care has been developed from these courses (Puchalski et al. 2006). This model defines two major components of spiritual care: an extrinsic one, which includes taking a spiritual history and incorporating patients' spiritual beliefs and values appropriately into treatment, and an intrinsic one, which focuses on the relationship aspect of the caregiver-patient interaction. This later aspect is centered on compassionate loving presence with the patient.

This model can also be applied to patients with dementia. However, there has been some controversy among religious leaders as to whether religious care can indeed be provided. The belief that dementia destroys personhood has also had an effect on how religious and pastoral caregivers view the religious life of patients with dementia. If there is "no person," then is there any need for the religious or spiritual aspect — that is, if the person cannot understand cognitively the ritual or the spiritual practice? Historically, it was thought that the capacity to take part fully in religious practice was lost in people with dementia (Power 2006). Bryden (2005), as a person with dementia, wrote that her faith and spiritual beliefs were essential to her well-being even when her cognitive and emotional self were impaired. She noted that it was important for others to connect with her faith. Shamy (2003), a pastoral caregiver, argues that when the brain fails, God is known to people in the heart. She has witnessed people with dementia experiencing a spiritual wisdom hours before death.

I have had similar experiences with my patients. The way I have witnessed it has not been through logic and intellect but through the spiritual connections I have formed with my patients — as well as what I have formed with my mother. The heart is the ultimate seat of God, or the Ultimate (however one understands that), and spirituality is grounded in the loving connections we form with each other and with God, the holy, or the divine. In order to provide excellent care for people with dementia, we must reframe what we value as significant. Power notes that "an understanding of personhood which values the non-rational is vital if we are to nurture spiritually a person with failing cognitive powers." Nonverbal connections, intuition, and presence are key elements of good care.

Ministry of Presence

The first step toward good care is the recognition of the spiritual aspect of the total care of the patient; therefore, focusing on the relationship that one forms with the persons with dementia is the first step. That relationship is based on a connection that transcends words and intellect. This first begins with the intention on the part of the caregiver, either a professional or a family member, to be fully present to the person with dementia. The second is to recognize the inherent value and dignity of that person regardless of his or her cognitive functioning. The third is to let go of preconceived notions as to what makes sense in conversations and interactions and to be open to letting intuition guide the caregiver in knowing what to do next.

Communication: Extrinsic Spiritual Care

A difficulty for many caregivers in communicating with people with dementia is that so much emphasis in our culture has been placed on a recall of the past. In the Judaeo-Christian tradition, faith is based on recalling events and interpreting those events in the context of human history. Religious rituals often celebrate an event from the past, for example, remembering how Jesus broke the bread at the Last Supper or how Moses led his people out of the desert. Stories make up a great deal of a community's faith experience. Goldsmith (1999) suggests that if one is to emphasize remembering God to a person with dementia, that person may not be able to connect with the faith being expressed; but by emphasizing that God remembers the person with dementia, that makes faith real for that person. In the medical model, doctors and nurses ask the patients about how they have been doing since the last visit. But people with dementia may not remember. Therefore, it is important to frame the visit within the present moment. It is similar for family caregivers: conversations that begin with "Do you remember?" may make the person feel more isolated. On the other hand, relating to the moment — using all one's senses to experience what is happening in the moment — helps to form connections. Then one can connect present emotions to stories of the past. When the person with dementia feels a warm embrace, the family member can bring up images of the past — a hug at a birthday party, the nuzzle of a family pet from the past, or simply a statement about the love shared over many years. At times that may help the person remember experiences and feelings independent of details.

Part of the extrinsic aspect of spiritual care is communicating with patients about spiritual beliefs and practices and what gives their life meaning. This may not be possible for the person with dementia, but one can talk with family and friends about what they know about the person. Storytelling in the presence of the person with dementia may be one way to honor the life of that person. One can also listen to the person for spiritual or religious themes and for aspects of life that may be meaningful still for that person.

Music has been used in many settings to calm people; interestingly, it has also been used to trigger reminiscences in older people with dementia (Dopson 2005). Hence, while verbal reminiscences of the past may not work with people with dementia, music or art or poetry may be contexts in which people can remember in different ways. Spiritual rituals such as prayer, music, sacraments, readings, use of the rosary, accompanying the person to a worship service, and other rituals, may result in decreased anxiety and stress for the patient (Mooney 2006). Rituals touch the person at an emotional level and may help that person come alive from her heart even when her mental faculties are failing. Rituals are an external expression, often in community, of deep spiritual longings and beliefs.

Spiritual Formation for the Caregiver

We have so much to learn from those for whom we care. That learning can become a process of spiritual formation for the caregiver. By being open to the mystery of what may happen in the present moment with people with dementia, caregivers may find some new meaning and purpose in their own lives. They may find a renewed sense of who they are with respect to their loved one or their patient. Rather than trying to control situations that are not controllable or predictable, caregivers can relax in the moment and relieve themselves of the worry and stress that often accompanies the care of someone with dementia. The caregiver can sit in silence and experience the wholeness of the other. As Mother Teresa (2007) said, "We need silence to be able to touch souls." There can be room for joy, meaning, and hope in the midst of what may seem like total darkness.

The Essence of Humanity: The Spirit

The key, I believe, in caring for people with dementia is to look at the very nature of how we see the essence of the human being. On one level, that essence may be imbued with social status, accomplishments, physical prowess, and mental acuity. In such a definition there is no room for frailties. But as people age or become seriously ill, those activities and relationships that gave meaning to their sense of who they are begin to fall apart. Therefore, as people begin to face their mortality, profound questions arise about the meaning of their lives, who they are, and what the purpose of life has been (Puchalski 2006). It is often in the setting of dying that people begin to look at themselves in new ways and to search for that profound understanding of who they are at their spiritual core, with all the frailties and with very few of the defenses they used all their lives to detach from or avoid the frailties. In illnesses and aging where cognition is for the most part intact, this journey often involves an intellectual processing of what is happening to the aging person; in some ways those aging persons can still hold onto some level of control and protection. People with dementia have no choice but to face that search for deep meaning: not only are their physical capacities diminished, and their relationships changed, but they even begin to lose the memories and definitions that gave them support and comfort all their lives. They are forced to become naked and exposed, with no defenses and no support, no history, no future — just the present moment.

Dementia is the ultimate dark night of the soul. Saint John of the Cross writes of the dark night as an experience that forces us to reconsider old beliefs and values about life, about ourselves, and about God (St. John of the Cross 1991). The deeply held understandings of life's supposed realities fall away as we go deeper within to find that real essence. There is a gradual process of detachment from the externals to allow a visioning of the divine within each of us. Ewing (2005) suggests that memory loss "might be the beginning of steps towards nurturing spiritual life."

In the silence of dementia, there may be an understanding, though not cognitive, and new meaning of one's self that transcends the usual meanings. Mother Teresa (2007) speaks of the wisdom of silence in this statement: "We need to find God, and He cannot be found in noise and restlessness. God is the friend of silence." Most spiritual traditions write of the importance of silence as a way to achieve a deeper understanding of the divine or the inner essence. Dementia imposes that silence, though it is not, of course, voluntary. This could be considered the passive purification that Saint John speaks of in "The Dark Night of the Soul." Passive purification indicates the nonvoluntary diminishment of our abilities — be they physical, intellectual, or emotional — that we undergo in the aging process. This diminishment creates in people with dementia the awareness that they are not in total control of their lives. The purification can lead to a letting go of the illusions of control and toward a greater dependence on God, or the divine, for our future. For people with dementia, this process of letting go can begin early in the course of the disease and extend to the point where they have no cognitive awareness.

In his famous poem, Saint John refers to our "house being stilled" as we move deeper into contemplation. In that still house we can see "the Beloved," or God.

> One dark night,
> Fired with love's urgent longings
> — ah, the sheer grace
> I went out unseen.
> My house being now all stilled. . . .
> I abandoned and forgot myself
> Laying my face on my Beloved;
> All things ceased; I went out from myself,
> Leaving my cares
> Forgotten among the lilies.
>
> (St. John of the Cross 1991, 50-52)

People with dementia have their houses stilled. What we may see as nothingness may actually be a kind of deep contemplation or a spiritual state that is, as yet, beyond our understanding. In that place they are touching God, or the divine, or the inner essence. By entering into that space with them, we may glimpse that holy reality as well. Working with and caring for people with dementia is thus spiritual formation for the caregivers.

One day I was at a lake with my mother. We sat in the sun looking at the lilies, the ducks, and the flowers around us. But I was only partially looking at those things. I was looking at my mother, quiet, still — not even answering my questions. I started worrying that her illness was progressing, that her mental status was declining, and that soon there might be no conversation between us. In my highest moment of anticipatory grief and anxiety, my mother gently laid her hand on my lap and said, "Look around, aren't these flowers so beautiful and see the ducks. . . ." Though her words stopped, they were overshadowed by her spirit of gentleness, her calm, and her awareness beyond my comprehension. In that moment I felt God, I felt her, and I felt an immense love. In that moment I learned the meaning of living in the present moment. The cares of us both had left, forgotten among the lilies.

References

Alcoholics Anonymous World Services, Inc. 1976. *Alcoholics Anonymous.* New York.

Baines, E. 1984. Caregiver stress in the older adult. *Journal of Community Health Nursing* 4: 257-63.

Blank, J., L. Clark, A. Longman, and J. Atwood. 1991. Perceived home care needs of cancer patients and their caregivers. *Cancer Nursing* 12 (2): 78-84.

Brown, M., and G. Powell-Cope. 1991. AIDS family caregiving: Transitions through uncertainty. *Nursing Research* 40 (6): 338-45.

Bryden, C. 2005. *Dancing with dementia.* London: Kingsley.

Chang, B. H., A. Noonan, and S. Tennstedt. 1998. The role of religion/spirituality in coping with caregiving for disabled elders. *The Gerontologist* 38 (4): 463-70.

Cupertino, A.-P., C. Aldwin, and R. Schulz. 1998. *Religiosity, emotional strain, and health: The caregiver health effects study.* San Francisco: American Psychiatric Association.

Dopson, L. 2005. Soul music. *Nursing Older People* 17.

Ellison, G., and J. Levin. 1998. The religion-health connections: Evidence, theory, and future direction. *Health Education and Behavior* 25: 700-720.

Ewing, W. 2005. Land of forgiveness: Dementia care as spiritual formation. *Journal of Gerontological Social Work* 45 (3): 301-11.

Ferrans, C., and M. Powers. 1993. Quality of life of hemodialysis patients. *ANNA Journal* 18: 173-81.

Folkman, S., M. Chesney, M. Cooke, A. Boccellari, and L. Collette. 1994. Caregiving burden in HIV-positive and HIV-negative partners of men with AIDS. *Journal of Consulting and Clinical Psychology* 62: 746-56.

Forbes, E. 1994. Spirituality, aging, and the community-dwelling caregiver and care recipient. *Geriatric Nursing* 15 (6): 297-302.

Goldsmith, M. 1999. Dementia: A challenge to Christian theology and pastoral care. In *Spirituality and Aging*, ed. A. Jewell. London: Kingsley.

Jivanjee, P. 1994. Enhancing the well-being of family caregivers to patients of Alzheimer's disease. *Journal of Gerontological Social Work* 23 (12): 31-48.

Jones, P., X. Zhang, K. Jaceldo-Siegl, and A. Meleis. 2002. Caregiving between two cultures: An integrative experience. *Journal of Transcultural Nursing* 13 (3): 202-9.

Kaye, J., and K. Robinson. 1994. Spirituality among caregivers. *Journal of Nursing Scholarship* 26 (Fall): 218-21.

Kuhlman, G., H. Wilson, S. Hutchinson, and M. Wallhagen. 1991. Alzheimer's disease and family caregiving: Critical synthesis of the literature and research agenda. *Nursing Research* 40: 331-37.

Lindgren, C. 1993. The caregiver career. *Journal of Nursing Scholarship* 24: 214-19.

Mickley, J., K. Pargament, C. Brant, and K. Hipp. 1998. God and the search for meaning among hospice caregivers. *The Hospice Journal* 13 (4): 1-17.

Moloney, M. 1995. A Heideggerian hermeneutical analysis of older women's stories of being strong. *Journal of Nursing Scholarship* 27 (2): 104-9.

Mooney, S. 2006. When memory fails. *Journal of Christian Nursing* (Winter): 14.

Mother Teresa, quoted at: www.iloveindia.com/indian-heroes/mother-teresa/quote.html (accessed Jan. 20, 2007).

MSOP III Report AAMC. 1999. *Spiritual, cultural and end of life issues.* Washington DC: AAMC.

Pierce, L. 2001. Caring and expressions of spirituality by urban caregivers of people with stroke in African American families. *Qualitative Health Research* 11 (3): 339-52.

Power, J. 2006. Religious and spiritual care. *Nursing Older People* 18 (7).

Puchalski, C. M. 2006. *A time for listening and caring: Spirituality and the care of the chronically ill and dying.* New York: Oxford University Press.

Puchalski, C., B. Lunsford, M. Harris, and T. Miller. 2006. Interdisciplinary spiritual care for seriously ill and dying patients: A Collaborative Model. *The Cancer Journal* 12 (5): 398-416.

Reed, P. 1994. Response to "The relationship between spiritual perspective, social support, and depression in caregiving and non-caregiving wives." *Scholarly Inquiry for Nursing Practice* 8 (4): 391-97.

Richardson, R., and A. Sistler. 1999. The well-being of elderly black caregivers and noncaregivers: A preliminary study. *Journal of Gerontological Social Work* 31 (1/2): 109-17.

Segall, M., and M. Wykle. 1989. The black family's experience with dementia. *Journal of Applied Social Sciences* 13: 171-91.

Shamy, E. 2003. *A guide to the spiritual dimension of care for people with Alzheimer's disease and related dementia.* London: Kingsley.

St. John of the Cross. 1991. The dark night of the soul. In *The Collected Works of St. John of the Cross,* ed. K. Kavanaugh and O. Rodriguez. Washington, DC: ICS.

Sutcliff, D. 2001. *Introducing dementia: The essential facts and issues of care.* London: Age Concern England.

Chapter Four

Effects of Social Exclusion and Interpersonal Rejection: An Overview with Implications for Human Disability

Roy F. Baumeister

Exclusion from some social interactions may be a perennial problem for people who suffer from disabilities. This exclusion can take multiple forms and arise for multiple reasons. Some disabilities limit one's ability to participate in various spheres of human life, either by making social interactions impractical or simply by increasing the difficulty of getting oneself into some venues where people interact. Exclusion may also occur because other people hold negative attitudes and prejudices with regard to people with disabilities and thus prefer to avoid interacting with them. These attitudes may stem from awkwardness and uncertainty about how to act, or they may arise because people find the very presence of people with disabilities to be threatening reminders of their own potential vulnerability to physical suffering, incapacitation, and death. In many cases they may simply reflect the unfortunate but widespread human preference to interact with people who are healthy and attractive. Finally, exclusion may sometimes be partly or wholly self-imposed, insofar as people with disabilities may themselves avoid some kinds of social interaction for several reasons: because they dislike being the object of others' pity, or they fear rejection or other negative reactions, or because the persons with disabilities feel embarrassed or ashamed about their own incapacities.

The purpose of this brief essay is to review research on the effects of social exclusion and interpersonal rejection as conducted in my laboratory over the past decade. None of this work has directly examined exclusion among people with disabilities, but insofar as many of them regularly grapple with exclusion as a perennial experience and fact of their lives, this research may resonate with their problems. Rejection and exclusion are faced by a great many persons, abled and disabled, and it may thus be a sphere in which the broader community can profitably learn from disability and from those people who learn to cope with exclusion.

The methods we use to study social exclusion may help place our findings in context and make them easier to understand, and so I begin by quickly summarizing them. Most of our work involves young-adult research participants who initially have no inkling that they will suffer social exclusion or that that is the focus of the research. Typically, they sign up for an experiment advertised as dealing with group discussion or problem-solving processes. In one procedure, they arrive at the laboratory to find that they will be part of a group of strangers. They are asked to engage in a get-acquainted conversation for about ten minutes — ostensibly to help them get to know each other — in which they reveal standard information about themselves according to some explicit questions and prompts. After this, the experimenter says that the next phase of the experiment involves pairing off and that participants should list the two or three other group members with whom they would like to work. Then each individual is put into a separate room, and the experimenter comes around to meet them individually. In the crucial condition, the experimenter says that there has been an unforeseen problem: nobody in the group has chosen to work with you. The others are told that everyone has chosen to work with them, which has raised practical problems. Participants are thus randomly assigned to hear either that no one or everyone selected them as a desired interaction partner.

In another procedure, participants take what appears to be a personality test and receive some feedback about their scores. Along with their scores, the experimenter gives them an additional prediction about their future, ostensibly stemming from their test results. By purely random assignment, some are told that they are likely to end up alone in life, because their friendships and romantic relationships will prove ephemeral and as they get older they will cease to make new friends. Other participants are told that they will always be surrounded by people who love and care about them (future social belongingness); others are told that they will be accident prone and will suffer many physical injuries (misfortune control, which is relevant because it is bad news but not involving social exclusion); still others receive no such predictions at all (neutral, no-information control).

Readers will notice that these research procedures involve deceiving participants. Most professional researchers in social psychology rely on such deceptions, not because they enjoy deceiving people, but because there is no other way. One of the landmark events in the history of social science was the discovery of the so-called Hawthorne effect, which is that when people know some aspect of their behavior is being studied, that aspect changes. If we were to tell people that we are studying their reactions to randomly assigned rejection, and then reject them randomly, their reactions would likely be different from how people respond to actual rejection experiences. Modern social psychology was shaped by the seminal studies on conformity by Solomon Asch, studies that were presented to participants as research on perception. A group would sit in a room and make judgments about which of three lines matched another line in length. When participants were alone, they got 100 percent of the answers correct. However, Asch had told some members of the group that, on a prearranged signal, they should all give a particular wrong answer. One member of the group had not been previously told about the signal, and the point of the experiment was to see whether that person would give the correct answer or would go along with the group by giving the same wrong answer that everyone else did. Obviously, this experiment would have been pointless had the experimenter explained to that person in advance that "from time to time, everyone else will give a wrong answer, and we want to see whether you say what you can see is obviously correct or just go along with everybody else in stating something that is not true."

Deception is, of course, hardly unique to research. In ordinary life we frequently deceive another person, not for the sake of deception but to help that person feel better about himself or herself. One important feature of deception in research, however, is that researchers are very careful to ensure that deceptions are temporary and that no harm is done to the hearers. All procedures are carefully reviewed by an ethics panel. All participants are told that they do not have to complete any procedure and can terminate at any time. And as soon as the data are collected, researchers explain the procedures and reveal the deceptions, so that nobody ever leaves the laboratory still believing that he or she was rejected. (In other words, subjects of the experiment are in a state of being deceived for only a few minutes.) We fully explain the rationale for the deception, and in my laboratory I also encourage experimenters to apologize for the deception. If anyone is upset about any aspect of the procedure, including the deception (or anything else), we encourage him or her to contact the professor in charge or file a complaint, and we also make available the option of receiving counseling.

Fortunately, such negative reactions are extremely rare. Most research participants readily understand the importance of studying such phenomena as social rejection and likewise understand the need for deception in order to make the experience seem real so that authentic responses can be observed. At this point we have run literally thousands of participants (generally college students) through these procedures without harm. Given the careful explanations that we administer at the end of the session, most leave with a feeling that they learned something about themselves and about psychology, are relieved that they were not really rejected, and have a feeling that they have had an interesting experience.

We use two other procedures occasionally. In one, a participant meets another person, and they exchange videotaped messages; one of them is then told that the other person left the experiment, either because of a negative reaction to what he or she learned about the other participant, or because he or she just remembered a physician appointment and needed to leave immediately. In the other procedure, the so-called cyber ball procedure, people play an online computer version of Frisbee or catch with some other participants, who gradually stop including the subject and just throw the Frisbee or ball back and forth between themselves.

Following these manipulations, we measure how people react — indeed, how they act — in a new, supposedly unrelated situation. In our first studies, for example, we had people move on to an ostensibly new experiment in which they were to write a brief essay, receive criticism or praise, and then play a game with a new person. The game contained the opportunity to behave aggressively toward the other person by delivering loud blasts of stressful, aversive noise. We found that excluded people were more aggressive toward the new person, unless that person had praised them quite strongly (Twenge et al. 2001). Thus social exclusion made people more aggressive. More recent work has found that the excluded people are less prone to cooperate with others or behave in generous, helpful, prosocial ways (Twenge et al. 2007).

One might think (as we certainly did) that the behavioral reactions of excluded people would show emotional distress. Hearing descriptions of our procedures is often enough to make people feel sorry for those who undergo the rejection manipulations, and most people intuitively predict that participants who were excluded would quickly become very upset. Yet one of the most surprising findings from this work has been the lack of emotional reaction. In study after study, we have rather consistently found that people report very little emotional feeling in response to these rejection manipulations. If they do feel less positive than do those in the accepted conditions (an occasional result), it is because the accepted participants feel good and happy, while the rejected ones continue to report neutral emotional states.

Over time we have begun to establish what happens instead of the wave of emotional distress we might have predicted. It appears that the first reaction to being rejected is to go numb. In fact, this numbness appears to be both physical and emotional. It may be related to the physical shock reaction that occurs when people or animals suffer an injury. Animals in the wild who are excluded from their social groups lose some of their sensitivity to pain (MacDonald and Leary 2005). Human beings in the laboratory apparently have the same reaction. In one series of studies, we confirmed that our manipulations made people less reactive to physical pain, such that they tolerated much more intense physical stimulation before they found it painful and before it was intolerable, as compared to participants in other conditions (DeWall and Baumeister 2006). Of course, we carefully chose the pain apparatus to be safe and harmless, and all participants were reminded that they did not have to tolerate any stimulation at all. But many people are interested in testing their tolerance to pain, which is done by putting pressure on the fingertip. The study of human pain tolerance is an important research area in its own right, and the technology has advanced so that it can be studied safely and effectively.

Moreover, the loss of feeling of physical pain went hand in hand with a loss of emotional sensitivity. Even when we asked subjects for their emotional reactions that had nothing to do with their recent laboratory-administered rejection experience, they seemed emotionally numb. We asked people in one study to forecast how they would react to a loss or victory by their university's football team in a big game scheduled for the following month. Most students predicted strong reactions; but those who had recently been excluded in our experiments predicted mild responses, suggesting that they would not care much either way. In other studies, we asked subjects to empathize with a fellow student who had either suffered a romantic breakup or a physical injury, and again the rejected ones lacked most signs of sympathy or concern toward the other person. The more numb they were to physical pain, the less emotional empathy they felt toward others (DeWall and Baumeister 2006).

What we think happens is that social exclusion produces a numbing response, possibly mediated by the internal release of opioids. These make the person lose sensitivity both to physical pain and to emotional reactions, but the person does not necessarily realize that he or she has gone numb in this way. Emotional empathy is an important tool for understanding other people and getting along with them, and so rejected people seem to lose this tool and hence lose part of their ability to understand and get along with others. This is one reason they cease to be helpful to others in need: they are unable to sympathize with the problems and needs of others, and so they do not feel like helping (Twenge et al. 2007).

These processes may create unrecognized further problems for the person with disabilities or, indeed, for anyone who experiences social exclusion. The rejection creates a state that makes the person less able to respond emotionally and less able to use his or her own emotions to understand others. Hence, further social interactions are complicated and may not go well, potentially creating a vicious circle in which unsatisfying social interactions bring further rejections.

Repeated experiences of social exclusion may each produce similar numbing reactions, but as these accumulate over time, they could eventually weaken the body's ability to cope by releasing opioids. If so, then over time the body might become less able to defend itself against new physical sources of pain. We do have some evidence relevant to this. People who report having suffered more social exclusion and rejection during childhood seem to suffer more troubling pain in adulthood, even if we hold the illnesses and injuries constant (DeWall and Baumeister 2006). This is not a matter of current pain causing people to remember more childhood rejection experiences; rather, the childhood rejections apparently lead to more pain in adulthood.

The numbness response takes on an added dimension of tragedy insofar as rejected people often really do want to find acceptance. The increased aggression, reduced helpfulness, and reduced empathy may give the impression that rejected people have decided to turn their backs on other people or crawl into an isolated shell. In fact, however, they want to connect. For rejected people, however, any urge to find new relationship partners is tempered by a reluctance to expose themselves to additional rejection. They are thus wary and cautious about approaching others. In another recent series of studies (Maner et al. 2007), we found that rejected persons were more eager than others to interact, distribute rewards, or meet new people, provided that this was set in a context where they had little or no risk of being rejected again. When the other makes the first move, they may be willing and even eager to respond; but they lack the basic trust that enables many people who have not been rejected to approach others and initiate an interaction.

The emotional numbness that stems from being rejected is not the only relevant inner response. We have identified several others, though it is possible that they are all interrelated in some ways. One area of deficiency is in intellectual performance. Rejected people become temporarily less intelligent than others, on average; in fact, the temporary drop in IQ is fairly substantial. Simple information-processing abilities such as comprehension and rote memory are unaffected, but complex abilities such as logical reasoning, extrapolation, and inference exhibit pronounced impairments (Baumeister et al. 2002). Another area of impairment is in self-control or self-regulation (Baumeister et al. 2005). Rejected people tend to behave in relatively shortsighted, impulsive, undisciplined ways. These patterns encompass not only selfish actions but also attention control and the ability to concentrate, such as when one must screen out distractions to focus on the task at hand.

Actually, our findings suggest that the self-regulation problem is a matter of being unwilling rather than unable to control the self, because we have found that rejected people are able to exert self-control when they have a compelling (usually self-interested) reason to do so. Our current theory is that self-control essentially is a difficult, somewhat aversive exertion, which people are generally willing to make as part of a social contract in which they conform to social norms, rules, and expectations in exchange for receiving the benefits of belongingness. Therefore, when people find themselves rejected, they feel that the contract has been violated, and they lose the inclination to make the exertions and sacrifices that self-control entails.

The impairment in self-control is linked to a reduction in self-awareness. Socially excluded people prefer to avoid being aware of themselves. In one study, for example, the manipulation of a lonely or socially accepted future was followed by an instruction to enter a room and take a seat, and the seats were distributed so that some faced toward walls with mirrors, others away from them. Obviously, mirrors focus attention on the self. The socially excluded persons were much more likely than others to choose the seats facing away from the mirrors (Twenge at al. 2003). Clearly, this pattern might also apply to persons with disabilities: they may very well find it aversive to focus attention on their handicapped bodies just after someone has rejected or excluded them. Self-awareness is an important component of self-regulation; thus, when people avoid self-awareness, they cannot self-regulate as effectively. When excluded people are made to focus on themselves, such as by the presence of a mirror, their self-control improves, even in spheres for which the mirror image of self is logically irrelevant (Baumeister et al. 2005).

A final area of behavioral change that we have observed in excluded persons is a rise in self-defeating behavior (Twenge et al. 2002). Classic theories of self-defeating and self-destructive behaviors have attributed them to negative attitudes about the self, such as self-dislike or desire for punishment, but these have largely been discredited. Instead, most self-defeating patterns conform to the pattern of long-term costs tied to short-term benefits or other seductive tradeoffs (see Baumeister 1997; Baumeister and Scher 1988). Poor self-control is often associated with these, insofar as people focus on immediate gratification and fail to consider or to follow the contingencies for enlightened self-interest. When people are struggling to avoid feeling bad, they sometimes lean toward actions that promise immediate relief or benefits, even at the potential cost of delayed problems or heightened risks (Tice et al. 2001).

In this paper I have offered an introductory overview of what we know about the impact of social exclusion and rejection on normally abled people. People with disabilities may encounter experiences of rejection and social exclusion from time to time, and sometimes unexpectedly, and so they may be at risk for these same effects. Given their fairly substantial potential costs — physical and emotional numbness, impaired intellectual functioning, failures at self-control, possible self-defeating behavior patterns, and the rest — it seems possible that people who are exposed to a frequent risk of these responses would learn to cope in more constructive ways in order to minimize the negative impact. If we can learn from persons with disabilities how they accomplish this, it would be a valuable lesson for all humankind.

On the other hand, it may often be true that prolonged experiences of exclusion seem to solidify the negative effects of the kind we have found in our laboratory studies, as is suggested in Jean Vanier's essay in this book. One useful implication may be that many unattractive features of disabled persons are not properties of these persons per se but rather secondary results of chronic rejection and exclusion. When such individuals can be made to feel accepted, such as in communities like L'Arche, these negative effects of rejection can be reduced or even reversed (see following chapter).

References

Baumeister, R. F. 1997. Esteem threat, self-regulatory breakdown, and emotional distress as factors in self-defeating behavior. *Review of General Psychology* 1: 145-74.

————. 2005. Rejected and alone. *The Psychologist* 18: 732-35.

Baumeister, R. F., C. N. DeWall, N. J. Ciarocco, and J. M. Twenge. 2005. Social exclusion impairs self-regulation. *Journal of Personality and Social Psychology* 88: 589-604.

Baumeister, R. F., and S. J. Scher. 1988. Self-defeating behavior patterns among normal individuals: Review and analysis of common self-destructive tendencies. *Psychological Bulletin* 104: 3-22.

Baumeister, R. F., J. M. Twenge, and C. Nuss. 2002. Effects of social exclusion on cognitive processes: Anticipated aloneness reduces intelligent thought. *Journal of Personality and Social Psychology* 83: 817-27.

DeWall, C. N., and R. F. Baumeister. 2006. Alone but feeling no pain: Effects of social exclusion on physical pain tolerance and pain threshold, affective forecasting, and interpersonal empathy. *Journal of Personality and Social Psychology* 91: 1-15.

Maner, J. K., C. N. DeWall, R. F. Baumeister, and M. Schaller. 2007. Does social exclusion motivate interpersonal reconnection? Resolving the "porcupine problem." *Journal of Personality and Social Psychology* 92: 42-55.

Tice, D. M., E. Bratslavsky, and R. F. Baumeister. 2001. Emotional distress regulation takes precedence over impulse control: If you feel bad, do it! *Journal of Personality and Social Psychology* 80: 53-67.

Twenge, J. M., R. F. Baumeister, D. M. Tice, and T. S. Stucke. 2001. If you can't join them, beat them: Effects of social exclusion on aggressive behavior. *Journal of Personality and Social Psychology* 81: 1058-69.

Twenge, J. M., K. R. Catanese, and R. F. Baumeister. 2002. Social exclusion causes self-defeating behavior. *Journal of Personality and Social Psychology* 83: 606-15.

Twenge, J. M., K. R. Catanese, and R. F. Baumeister. 2003. Social exclusion and the deconstructed state: Time perception, meaninglessness, lethargy, lack of emotion, and self-awareness. *Journal of Personality and Social Psychology* 85: 409-23.

Twenge, J. M., R. F. Baumeister, C. N. DeWall, N. J. Ciarocco, and J. M. Bartels. 2007. Social exclusion decreases prosocial behavior. *Journal of Personality and Social Psychology* 92: 56-66.

Chapter Five

Moral Transformation in L'Arche Communities for People with Developmental Disabilities

KEVIN S. REIMER

Our mission is to create homes where faithful relationships based on forgiveness and celebration are nurtured. We want to reveal the unique value and vocation of each person, and to live relationships in community as a sign of hope and love.

L'Arche Charter

Introduction

The house was old, with heavy beams but newly painted trim. I rang the bell and was greeted by my interview participant, a woman in middle age with flowing hair and limpid eyes. The home was not her own but rather that of a community of persons with disabilities living with their caregivers, known as L'Arche. As we walked through the house, our steps echoed in cadence with noises upstairs from a nonverbal resident. My hostess, a highly regarded caregiver for nearly a decade in this home, ushered me into a tiny office. While she made tea, I scanned the walls, which were filled with pictures of

This social scientific study of human altruism in American L'Arche communities was made possible with a grant from the John Fetzer Institute (#1653.8). I am grateful for the friendship of leaders and community members from L'Arche USA, who made the project a reality. The research focused on the development of altruistic commitment in L'Arche caregiver assistants. I have changed or removed identifying information to protect the identities of L'Arche caregivers, core members, and their communities.

community members at picnics and birthday parties. These were spontane-ous family portraits that celebrated people's achievements. The smiles were unforced, the relationships authentic. I chatted with the caregiver about the pictures. At some point our conversation crossed that thin line between ca-sual exchange and the formality of a research interview. But, somewhat to my surprise, our conversation continually referred to the family photos that surrounded us. The reasons for this became clearer as we discussed the deeper meaning of her work with people with developmental disabilities.

I was raped in high school. Even though my family moved around a lot and there was a lot of suffering and isolation, as a people person I was able to fit in and make friends quickly — even when I was dying inside. After the rape I gained thirty pounds; I probably became severely de-pressed, severely dissociated. This was an insane time. I never told any-body. My junior and senior year of high school I didn't have a single friend. There were some people I socialized with a little bit at school. I went from being someone who dated to someone who was overweight, invisible, severely depressed — and nobody noticed. If I let myself re-enter it, the pain was huge. What it gave me was that I experienced what it was like to be entirely on the outside looking in. And things looked really different that way. I think it brought me to a whole different level. It's interesting, I had a lot of feeling for people who were on the outside. I was the kind of kid who couldn't stand people being picked on. But I hadn't been completely that way. I just felt ugly and awful and icky. It was humiliating. I can still remember not having a date for my prom. Or not going to a single dance. But I think it gave me a whole experience of being a part of a world.

How did this relate to L'Arche?

I look at the core members. I mean, what more rejected group is there? What group wears their pain in such a manner? Not that anybody should be ashamed, but let's face it: most people who are handicapped feel shame. And they wear it. To feel voiceless, to feel invisible, to feel un-attractive. I used to think, I'll never get married. No man could ever love me. I've dwelt in the shadow lands. But I think it impacted receptivity in my heart. Much of that wasn't at a conscious level or awakening my own experience. That came later, over the years. I think I've been much more freed up at L'Arche. It's impacted my ability to be more forgiving. I think the community allows people to be free. I think it's a movement into more freedom, more joy, more peace, more tolerance for other people. I get less worried about things now. I feel like, I've always said God will provide, but now I'm living in it more.

It was a remarkable moment. Despite acute pain, her gestures were continually directed toward the family pictures on the wall. Our conversation was framed by a host of individuals with disabilities who understood the contours of rejection and suffering, but also the possibility of realized worth. Her time in L'Arche resulted in tangible recovery from shame.

From this encounter and others, I contend that the wisdom of disability in L'Arche is that shame can be transformed into other-oriented moral maturity, which may include capacities for sound moral judgment, agency, empathy, perspective-taking, and altruistic love or compassionate care (Balswick et al. 2005). My purpose in this chapter is to consider recovery from shame as part of moral transformation. This woman's development is bounded by community: instances of relationship with core members that alter self-understanding from a posture of rejection to acceptance.[1] Development is instantiated through a shift in her experience of self toward socially adaptive outcomes marked by trust. Accordingly, I have organized this chapter around three guideposts from psychology that are relevant to developmental transition from shame to moral maturity.[2] These include moral *intuition, emotions,* and *self.* Because the discussion arises from the context of L'Arche, I will assume that moral transformation is an artifact of community, where relationships influence change from the level of behavior abstractions such as morality all the way down to neurological benchmarks. This is hardly a linear process. L'Arche members are the first to note developmental shortcomings associated with their own emotional wounds. Paradoxically, it is in this acknowledgment that moral transformation becomes a possibility (see Vanier, chap. 1 above).

The L'Arche Conundrum

The legacy of L'Arche is that everyone experiences disability but remains worthy of dignity and unqualified respect. Core members provide instruc-

---

1. My use of the word "self" is constrained by relationship and social context.

2. I believe that moral transformation as experienced by the caregiver is multifaceted and complex. This essay is meant to provide a psychological complement to theological and philosophical insights regarding disability, an invitation to dialogue rather than a claim to exclusive understanding.

tion about how to live with disability. They must regularly contend with shame that comes with social stigmatization, and from these experiences core members know suffering profoundly. Many have histories involving the cruelty and abuse they suffered in institutional settings. Through a variety of circumstances they have come to live in L'Arche, where reconciliation and healing become real possibilities. For some, the transition comes easily; others require extended time to rehabilitate the trust necessary to function within community. In my interviews with some eighty L'Arche caregivers, they showed how they regarded core members as sources of inspiration: the latter modeled quiet triumph over shame. Dozens of caregivers pointed to the extraordinary resilience of core members. Caregivers also frequently aligned their narratives with examples of core members, recounting personal shame "disability" in the form of grievances, broken relationships, and interpersonal shortcomings. As was illustrated in my interview transcript, recognition of shame in the safety of L'Arche may reorder self-understanding toward other-oriented moral maturity.

In L'Arche, cognitively disabled core members are a primary catalyst in the transformation of caregivers. This unexpected path of influence creates a conundrum for the majority cohort of contemporary moral psychologists. For decades the field emphasized the development of moral maturity in *rationalism,* an agenda that reached its apex in the landmark theory of Lawrence Kohlberg, which has continued to demonstrate impressive durability and has influenced a generation of practitioners in education, psychology, and public policy (Kohlberg 1984).

Kohlberg's work upheld a morality tightly constrained to justice reasoning. Beginning with studies he conducted at Harvard in the 1960s and 1970s, Kohlberg outlined the developmental progression of justice reasoning through childhood, adolescence, and adulthood. The principal method of assessing change was the use of intractable moral dilemmas, a well-known example of which is the "Heinz dilemma," in which an unfortunate man must decide whether to steal an expensive cancer drug in order to save his dying spouse. Kohlberg analyzed dilemma responses in order to characterize depth and coherence in participant reasoning. Results from these studies were systematized into a stage-like framework for moral development, culminating in a dilemma-busting "universal" ethic at stage six. Moral maturity in the scheme is unavoidably cognitive, premised on a capacity for rational abstraction such that progressively fewer individuals achieve ethical mountaintops in stages five and six. Core members lacking sophisticated capacities for Kantian justice reasoning score at the lower levels of the moral stage framework. In this rationalist scheme, it is highly improbable that core L'Arche members would consistently inspire moral maturity in caregivers.

This overview implies two contingencies: either L'Arche caregivers are overstating the significance of core members in catalyzing moral transformation, or rationalist definitions of morality are narrow enough as to exclude the real-world moral experience of these individuals. The first contingency raises questions regarding caregiver motives. Why would caregivers overstate the role of core-member influence on deeply personal moral issues? One possible explanation arises from *social desirability bias*. Briefly, the psychological literature demonstrates that participants in survey or interview settings will align their attitudes with perceived researcher intentions. This effect is often cited by researchers as a justification for using deception in controlled experimental settings (see Baumeister, preceding chap.) Social desirability bias is a risk in semistructured interviews such as the one documented at the outset of this chapter. However, it seems remote that caregivers would consistently perceive that a researcher from outside L'Arche would understand and embrace the idea that people with disabilities serve as moral guides in recovery from shame. Social desirability bias tends to be premised on simpler and less controversial perceptions. Typical examples include a desire to withhold racial prejudice, underreporting risky sexual behavior, or exaggerating one's generosity through charitable giving.

The second contingency seems more plausible, namely, that the rationalist interpretation of morality provides an insufficient vantage from which to understand transformation in the caregiver narrative (Walker and Reimer 2005). L'Arche is a community with a particular moral vision that is rooted in Roman Catholic spirituality and Aristotelian virtue. L'Arche is a place with intellectual asymmetries, a place where people must learn to live with a startling range of cognitive diversity. Moral transformation in this environment is relatively unconcerned with abstraction; instead, it is given to the immediate relational and physical requirements of community life. Core members offer moral instruction that is deeply embedded in action and experience, much of which eschews deliberative reasoning or calculation. Core members may love others deeply, demonstrate great patience, or regularly extend forgiveness. Yet, when they are called upon to answer the question of why this is true, they often struggle to provide rational explanation. The challenge is to consider caregiver experience of moral transformation influenced by unexpected sources (e.g., core members) and directed toward earthy outcomes in character. This requires a moral psychology that affirms a broad horizon for experience that includes cognitive diversity. Accordingly, in this discussion I will briefly focus on guideposts of moral *intuition, emotion,* and *self,* which are consolidated into the capacity for trust.

Moral Intuitions

The caregiver interview offers clues regarding the nature of moral transformation in L'Arche. The woman I first interviewed acknowledges that the process didn't initially happen at a conscious level, or "awakening my own experience." That came later — over the years. Her awareness of moving from shame to moral maturity arises gradually. Maturation isn't precipitated on the basis of grand insight or didactic instruction. Forgiveness becomes slowly established in the context of newly discovered freedom in L'Arche. Her experience is consistent with Jonathan Haidt's argument for morality premised on intuitions that function as evaluative feelings at the edge of consciousness (Haidt and Bjorklund 2008). Moral intuitions frame our perceptions of social situations and behaviors, helping us regulate morally charged circumstances on the basis of like-dislike or good-bad polarities. Disgust is a primary emotion supporting these intuitions (Haidt 2007). Haidt's *social intuitionist model* (SIM) of moral maturity does not eliminate deliberative moral reasoning. Instead, reasoning is reliant on a diverse range of intuitions catalogued in memory that provide us with emotional attenuation akin to "gut feeling" (Reimer 2003).

The intuitionist model assumes that the vast majority of moral functioning is characterized by situations requiring rapid appraisals and responses beneath consciousness. Moral intuitions are at work for the grade-school boy who spots a friend threatened by bullies on the playground and sprints to intervene. Intuitions are engaged by the trial lawyer who perceives character weaknesses in a witness and spontaneously redirects her cross-examination. Moral actions in these situations are predicated on quick, emotionally laden convictions of "rightness," rather than lengthy introspection. For Haidt, the bulk of real-world morality happens as an adaptive response to swiftly changing circumstances. Deliberative moral reasoning is comparatively less common, owing to its slow and methodical evaluation of future scenarios, consequences, and contingencies. Such deliberation requires significant allocation of cognitive resources. From the

SIM perspective, moral reasoning is a *post hoc* phenomenon, arising as a justification for intuition-driven decisions made rapidly and without extensive reflection. Intuitions comprise an adaptation that helped early hominids construct basic moral frameworks to govern social interactions. Deliberative moral reasoning is an evolutionary newcomer, reliant on more recent developments in the neocortex that effectively integrate older intuitive systems.

The social intuitionist model is accumulating an impressive record of scientific support, along with an equally impressive body of criticism, from rationalist researchers who excoriate the notion that reasoning relies on intuitions (Jacobsen 2008; Narvaez 2008).[3] Despite the dust cloud raised by the conflict, some elements of the SIM model may yet prove useful in helping us understand the role of core members in caregiver moral transformation. The emphasis on intuitions effectively levels the cognitive playing field with regard to a psychological understanding of moral maturation. Morality is no longer about one's ability to generate convincing moral diatribes on hypothetical dilemmas. Morality is instead about habit, or those elements of character that involve testing our lives against the well-lived lives of others (Hauerwas 1983). Habits are principally learned through example. Few would argue that many L'Arche core members live well, offering examples of compassionate love, generosity, and kindness that are instructive to others. Yet the moral force of core-member habits is not always characterized by deliberation or rationalization. In their affirmation of shame as a human experience, core members provide a powerful impetus for a moral maturity premised on habituated behaviors arising from emotional intuitions.

Moral Emotions

Strangely, there is no consideration of moral *emotions* as intuitions in the SIM model. Shame, guilt, and pride are well-known constituents in this class of emotions (Tangney 1999). Moral emotions make their debut in early childhood with maturation through adolescence and early adulthood

---

3. Because of space limitations, I cannot include the details of this debate here. A primary concern relates to Haidt's claim that moral reasoning is a *post hoc* phenomenon that justifies prior, intuition-driven behaviors. I agree with Haidt's critics, who point out that deliberative moral reasoning commonly precedes action in social information processing.

(Mascolo and Fischer 1995). *Shame* is understood as a paralyzing sense of defectiveness in the self. Shamed individuals feel exposed and humiliated, reflecting a social view of self as unworthy and disapproved. The caregiver I referred to at the beginning of this chapter provides a harrowing account of shame, an emotion that so completely defines her self-understanding that she is relegated to status as an outsider, living in a state of alienation from others. *Guilt* differs from shame in that the focus is given to specific actions rather than negative self-attributions. Guilty individuals experience remorse for behaviors and actively seek reparation through apology or other compensation. Together these so-called "negative" moral emotions marshal considerable influence over everyday behavior, constraining self-understanding and adaptation across a spectrum of social situations.

Taken together, shame and guilt are inversely related to the auspiciously "positive" moral emotion of *pride*. Pride is composed of two constituents. *Alpha* pride is the opposite of shame, offering a positive assessment of the self, recognizing intrinsic worth, and bestowing respect on self and others. Alpha pride is commonly found in the narratives of long-term caregivers at L'Arche.[4] *Beta* pride is the opposite of guilt in that it frames personal behaviors in a positive light. Beta pride refers to actions, such as praising a child who shares with a playmate, or praising a piano student who successfully completes a recital. It is important to note that both negative and positive emotions often co-occur, representing potentially complex intuitive information on the basis of social perceptions.

The moral implications of these emotions are widely recognized, particularly with regard to shame and guilt (Tangney 2002; Damon 1998). Moral emotions are known in studies of empathy: they are an important element in other-oriented maturity. Individuals mired in shame tend to exhibit empathy that is self-oriented or directed toward the needs of the empathizer rather than the sufferer. Tangney provides a telling example of this distorted caring: "It hurts *me* so much to see this happen to you!" (Tangney 1995). Conversely, guilt promotes other-oriented empathy that encourages sympathetic alignment of feeling between empathizer and sufferer, but it remains committed to the needs of the other. Guilt is clearly the more adaptive emotion on moral grounds, particularly when accompanied by moderate levels of alpha and beta pride. It is my contention that moral emotions provide a rich catalogue of social experiences as intuitions

---

4. This last conclusion is subjective: I have inferred it from forty interviews with long-term caregivers at L'Arche.

archived in memory. Moral emotion intuitions are therefore associated with specific, real-world actions. Such intuitions are more ethically substantive than aversive disgust as outlined in SIM. Unlike disgust, moral emotions are explicitly social and self-referential. Given the importance of self-worth in other-oriented care, moral emotions stand at a developmental crossroads of maturation potential.[5]

My introductory interview narrative provides a striking example of transition away from crippling shame. The caregiver recounts scenes of stark loneliness punctuated by humiliation and self-abasement. The narrative reflects a capacity for moral emotions to structure or organize the manner by which the caregiver perceives social situations and responds in kind. These perceptions critically involve core members who experience shame and reclaim dignity in their own process of moral maturation. The caregiver may witness a situation where a core member is pointedly ignored by a supermarket cashier in the checkout line. The caregiver identifies with the great pain of rejection that precipitates shame for the core member, but notes an unanticipated outcome in the core member's refusal to passively accept the situation, offering a stick of chewing gum to the cashier. The core member's response to a difficult situation upholds her worth as an individual and the potential for other-oriented care. For the observing caregiver, new combinations of moral intuitions are recorded in memory, available for similar situations in the future, which might directly involve the caregiver herself. This gradual "rewriting" of remembered scripts related to social contingencies and moral emotion intuitions is the basis for transformation.

What causes new moral emotion intuitions to stick? Rewritten scripts involving particular contingencies and intuitions can be expected to influence the caregiver's view of self over time. Our first interviewee's predispositions toward social situations and their moral requirements evolve from self-deprecation to the ratification of virtue in others and self. Responses emerging from altered predispositions result in different behavioral responses. Instead of life as a chronic outsider, this woman begins to engage others freely, no longer bound to external judgments of self as unworthy or ugly. Foundational to these changes is the caregiver's gradual move away

---

5. It is important to note that ethically satisfactory outcomes are less likely where moral emotions are singularly and excessively expressed. Overwhelming guilt is maladaptive without the counterbalancing influence of healthy pride. The inverse is also true, with chilling implications in sociopathy.

from shame as the emotional nexus of self-understanding and toward appraisals of the world premised on a more balanced ensemble of moral emotion intuitions.

Moral Self

Much of this discussion suggests pathways of moral influence from core member to caregiver that are preconscious. Moral emotion intuitions pack a considerable psychological punch, but they do their business with the subtlety of everyday routine, where change gradually reorders self-understanding through repeated encounter with similar social situations. To put it slightly differently, scripts are rewritten only after dozens or even hundreds of drafts. After several years in L'Arche, the above caregiver may learn that personal mistakes are permissible and even a cause for good-natured humor, as opposed to the prior shame from her family of origin. Guilt and pride intuitions begin to surface in the caregiver's appraisals of multiple mistakes, with forgiveness extended through community members. Revised appraisals provide a substrate for morally adaptive behavior, where the same caregiver learns to engage and forgive when wronged, a new action tendency that differs sharply from old responses such as avoidance. With this L'Arche caregiver, it is only after many repetitions of these encounters that she becomes aware of change at a level that permits reflection or a revised personal narrative that supports the emergence of a mature *moral self.*

Therefore, at some point, transformation from shame toward other-oriented maturity becomes a conscious aspect of self-understanding. The maturation of the moral self might be characterized in terms of consolidation, where intuition-based alterations to self-understanding are evidenced in the realization of goals that capture other-oriented moral priorities. The caregiver highlights forgiveness as an example of a newly realized goal that refers the self toward other-oriented outcomes. Forgiveness is consonant with the L'Arche context, a movement concerned with the communal practice of spiritual and Aristotelian virtues. Relationships between core members and caregivers provide opportunity to practice other-oriented moral goals. This is consistent with research findings that individuals nominated for the Nobel peace prize and other humanitarian awards pointed to close confidants in the formation of their personal goals (Colby and Damon 1992).

As with our L'Arche caregiver, consolidation of goals in self-understanding happened gradually for the Colby and Damon sample, where relationships forced a reevaluation of capacities and prompted new strategies to achieve moral objectives. In one example, a woman known for her care of people with disabilities shared how she began her career as an elementary school teacher. Because she needed work, a mentor encouraged her to take a job working with dyslexic children. In the context of the job, the mentor helped the woman to develop new skills and interests centered on the needs of people with disabilities. The experience of moral influence led to a complete restructuring of her personal goals concerning the care of those with profound disabilities.

The consolidation process is supported by biological evidence unearthed from an obscure chapter in American medical history. The renowned neurologist Antonio Damasio retells the sad story of Phineas Gage, a twenty-six-year-old railroad foreman in mid-nineteenth-century New England (Damasio 1994). Leading work crews through rugged country, Gage won a reputation as a conscientious boss who took personal interest in his men. Among his other talents, Gage was something of an expert in the use of blasting powder to ignite controlled explosions to remove rock and other natural barriers. Gage carried a specially designed iron rod for the purpose of tamping blasting powder. One unfortunate afternoon, he accidentally struck a piece of flint in a small bore hole filled with powder. The resulting explosion drove the iron rod completely through Gage's skull: it entered beneath the left cheekbone and exited through a small hole in the top of his head. Remarkably, Gage survived the accident. But it quickly became evident that Gage was no longer the same man. He couldn't make positive decisions regarding matters of relational and financial significance. Gage's cherished moral standards and work ethic disappeared. He could not hold down a job or execute the most basic plans. He became insolent and uncaring toward his fellows. Gage swiftly lost his fortune and left his wife and children for a life of promiscuity. He died as a circus-show freak some seventeen years later.

Damasio observes that Gage's injury was to the prefrontal cortex of the brain.[6] A close comparison of Gage's skull to similarly injured patients revealed grave trauma to the brain's central processor for emotion, the limbic system. The interesting thing to Damasio was that his contemporary patients evidenced many of Gage's symptoms. After their injuries, patients

---

6. An excellent overview of the moral neuroscience field is found in Moll et al. 2005.

failed to work conscientiously, were impaired in their ability to realize goals through planning and effort, had poor social skills, and were dramatically affected in moral functioning. Damasio's wife, Hanna, gave several of these patients Kohlberg's Heinz dilemma. The patients' responses to the dilemma were entirely normal, demonstrating conventional (stages 3 and 4) moral reasoning equivalent to a population without prefrontal brain injury. Yet, despite their solid capacity for moral reasoning, patients continued to struggle greatly in their attempts to achieve their personal goals; instead, they lived an uncaring and amoral existence (Damasio 2002).

Consolidation describes a maturing self that is consciously known on the basis of moral emotion intuitions in memory that serve as scaffolding for personal goals. The importance of a consolidated moral self to mature behavior is evident in the tragic examples of Gage and Damasio's prefrontal-cortex-damaged patients. Without a self that one knows on the basis of moral emotion intuitions, ethical reasoning is relegated to pedantic exercise. The absence of goals suggests that Gage and other patients were unable to weigh potentialities against past moral decisions, lacking subjective experience of how decisions leave one feeling during the days and weeks that follow. For maturing individuals such as our L'Arche caregiver, archived memories of moral emotion intuitions help keep goals in clear focus. She is able to recall past events situating the self in various social contexts, experiences marked with particular or combined moral emotion intuitions.[7] These memories permit her to weigh goals that were significant in the past with her present circumstances. Goal evaluation is emotion cued, and it may result in the alteration of her present goals based on past experience, present situation, and her ability to anticipate future outcomes. Transformation into other-oriented maturity reflects emotionally intuitive connections of social influences and experiences significant to the self.

Concluding Thoughts:
Trust and Maturity in the L'Arche Community

The L'Arche caregiver punctuates her narrative of moral transformation in noting personal freedom from shame. She is freed to live a life of moral in-

---

7. This recalls Damasio's argument for *somatic markers,* or embodied feelings that garner conscious moral attention (Damasio 1999, 184-85; see also Naqvi, Shiv, and Bechara 2006).

tegrity premised on respect for the self and the other. This requires trust. Trust is the finishing cement in maturity, solidifying change through consolidation of moral emotion intuitions into the self. The ongoing stability of the caregiver's character relies on her ability to trust others, to effectively sustain reciprocal exchange that makes goals such as forgiveness realistic and feasible.[8] Trust in this relational sense implicates bonding or *attachment,* a behavioral system that evolved to foster adaptive responses to social situations (Reimer 2005). Moral transformation is ultimately about change to the attachment behavioral system, which makes possible other-oriented commitments that begin with core member examples. An account of this process is evident in the caregiver narrative taken from another L'Arche community:

> I'll tell you a turning point in terms of my understanding of God and L'Arche. I was seeing the gifts of the core members. When I got to Tampico things were rough and I had to live in the house because we were so short of [caregiver] assistants. It was very difficult. One of the core members there was named Trent. He is blind and dual diagnosed. He was in an institution all his life, since a year old. I had this real love for Trent — a connection with him. I could calm him down, I enjoyed him. One night I was giving him his bath and I was drying off his back. He says, "You're my friend, right?" I stopped for a minute. What occurred? And yet he can love. He can still trust. . . . How many people didn't see this sacred life in front of them, just wanted to get the job [bathing him] done. How many times he had to put up with that. What he's really saying is, Can I trust you? Are you safe? Are you my friend? It occurred to me that this man probably lived through hell. Abuse. People being incredibly insensitive to him. I realized that I was in a transforming moment, knowing that I'm more broken than Trent. I could not be this vulnerable. I thought that I was being authentic but realized he was teaching me something that I hadn't learned. God was really present in that moment. That is when I could say that I didn't choose L'Arche but L'Arche has chosen me.

Moral transformation is effected in a mundane setting imbued with the potential for trust. Whatever the caregiver's experiences with close attach-

---

8. The stability of character or personality is not assumed across the behavioral sciences. Debate persists, particularly among neuroscientists and philosophers of mind.

ments prior to the encounter with Trent, it is obvious that the exchange rocked the foundations of her moral intuitions, emotions, and self. The fruit of moral transformation is found in the caregiver's renewed vision of compassionate love. Love in this instance is everyday and unpretentious. It is a love of the evening bath, vomit in the living room, and badly soiled underwear. Reciprocal exchange between caregiver and core member affirms mutual brokenness, bringing both together to find hope through a relationship with God. For Trent and his caregiver friend, trust grows where each comes clean regarding disability and limitation. Such trust is rocket fuel for the flourishing of other-oriented moral maturity.

References

Balswick, J. O., P. E. King, K. S. Reimer. 2005. *The reciprocating self: Human development in theological perspective.* Downers Grove, IL: InterVarsity.

Colby, A., and W. Damon. 1992. *Some do care: Contemporary lives of moral commitment.* New York: Free Press.

Damasio, A. 1994/2006. *Descartes' error.* New York: Vintage Books.

————. 1999. *The feeling of what happens.* New York: Harcourt.

Damasio, H. 2002. Impairment of interpersonal social behavior caused by acquired brain damage. In *Altruism and atruistic love: Science, philosophy, and religion in dialogue,* ed. S. Post, L. Underwood, J. Schloss, and W. Hurlbut, 264-71. New York: Oxford University Press.

Damon, W. 1998. *The moral child: Nurturing children's natural moral growth.* New York: Free Press.

Haidt, J. 2007. The new synthesis in moral psychology. *Science* 316: 998-1002.

Haidt, J., and F. Bjorklund. 2008. Social intuitionists answer six questions about moral psychology. In *Moral psychology,* ed. W. Sinnott-Armstrong, 3: 181-217. Cambridge, MA: MIT Bradford.

Hauerwas, S. M. 1983. *The peaceable kingdom: A primer in Christian ethics.* Notre Dame, IN: University of Notre Dame Press.

Jacobsen, D. 2008. Does social intuitionism flatter morality or challenge it? In *Moral Psychology,* ed. W. Sinott-Armstrong, 3: 219-32. Cambridge, MA: MIT Bradford.

Kohlberg, L. 1984. *Essays on moral development,* vol. 2: *The psychology of moral development.* San Francisco: Harper and Row.

Mascolo, M., and K. Fischer. 1995. Developmental transformations in appraisals for pride, shame, and guilt. In *Moral emotions: The psychology of shame, guilt, embarrassment, and pride,* ed. J. Tangney and K. Fischer, 64-113. New York: Guilford.

Moll, J., R. Zahn, R. De Oliveira-Souza, F. Krueger, and J. Grafman. 2005. The neural basis of human moral cognition. *Nature Reviews Neuroscience* 6: 799-809.

Narvaez, D. 2008. The social intuitionist model: Some counter-intuitions. In *Moral Psychology,* ed. W. Sinnott-Armstrong, 3: 233-40. Cambridge, MA: MIT Bradford.

Naqvi, N., B. Shiv, and A. Bechara. 2006. The role of emotion in decision making. *Current Directions in Psychological Science* 15: 260-63.

Reimer, K. S. 2003. Committed to caring: Transformation in adolescent moral identity. *Applied Developmental Science* 7: 129-37.

———. 2005. Revisiting moral attachment: Comment on identity and motivation. *Human Development* 48: 262-65.

Tangney, J. 1995. Shame and guilt in interpersonal relationships. In *Moral emotions: The psychology of shame, guilt, embarrassment, and pride,* ed. J. Tangney and K. Fischer, 114-39. New York: Guilford, 1995.

———. 1999. The moral emotions: Shame, guilt, embarrassment and pride. In *Handbook of Cognition and Emotion,* ed. T. Dalgleish and M. Power, 541-68. New York: John Wiley.

———. 2002. Moral emotions: The self as a moral guide. In *Self and motivation: Emerging psychological perspectives,* ed. A. Tessel, D. Stapel, and J. Wood, 97-117. Washington, DC: American Psychological Association.

Walker, L. J., and K. S. Reimer. 2005. The relationship between moral and spiritual development. In *The handbook of spiritual development in childhood and adolescence,* ed. P. Benson, P. King, L. Wagener, and E. Roehlkepartain, 265-301. Newbury Park, CA: Sage.

Chapter Six

Disability Attitudes, Cultural Conditions, and the Moral Imagination

PAMELA CUSHING

Introduction

It does not take much hunting to unearth signs that Western societies lack the imaginative resources for greater appreciation and inclusion of people with developmental disabilities. A recent newspaper series chronicles one family's decade of fighting to convince friends, professionals, and the state that their son deserves to be here. His father writes: "If I can prove Walker's broken presence is essential to the world, maybe someone will protect him when I'm no longer here to do so" (Brown 2007). I was not surprised to read, at the end of the series, that Walker's dad, Ian, a Toronto-based journalist, found inspiration in the work of Jean Vanier and L'Arche for how to love his son just as he is. Ian recounts how not all messages about his son were that encouraging: "If Walker is so insubstantial [to them], why does he feel so important to me?"

In this paper I assume that discrimination against people with developmental disabilities is partly rooted in the lack of cultural scripts that the general public has for experiencing or imagining them in positive ways, as fully human, and with gifts to share in friendships, families, and communities. While it remains an understudied area, emergent research indicating widespread loneliness, stress, and depression (Lunsky 2002; Harris 1991), as well as lack of friendships for people with developmental disabilities (Amado 1993), suggests that we are far from creating a welcoming society. In a pioneering Canadian survey on "being, belonging and becoming," the majority of people with developmental disabilities rated their quality of life as "poor to adequate" (Brown et al. 1997). It is increasingly clear that positive attitudes result neither automatically nor inevitably from mere exposure to people with disabilities in the community.

Against the background of these findings, I make the case that the communities of L'Arche create an alternative cultural setting in which caregivers' moral imagination regarding disability is greatly expanded. Living together in this milieu generates new ways of imagining the disabled other. I highlight key elements of their faith-based culture that create the conditions for this imaginative expansion, and I sketch the contours of what assistants are then able to learn from people with disabilities. The fact that L'Arche can nurture ordinary people's ability to imagine goodness in life with a disability is significant precisely because it is achieved against such a spare cultural backdrop. Indeed, Priestly prioritizes the need for research on "disabling cultural values" because so little is known (Priestly 2002).

As an anthropologist, my questions are: What are the cultural dimensions of L'Arche that cultivate the assistants' moral imagination in general, and particularly in recognizing the gifts of people with disabilities? What are some common lessons that assistants embody? My analysis is based on a year of intensive participant observation and nearly a hundred interviews in nine L'Arche communities across Canada in 1999-2000, as well as ongoing collaborations with those communities (Cushing 2003a). My subjects were current and former assistants (akin to caregivers or support workers) who varied in age, location, experience, and roles in their community. The engaged and extended nature of fieldwork provides anthropologists with special insight into people's messy daily reality and routines. Since 2000, my research with mainstream agencies, parent groups, and the Camphill schools has added to my understanding of the disability field.

What Vanier and other people connected with L'Arche have learned about mutual engagement with people with disabilities is not that devalued differences disappear, but that in a supportive environment most of those differences can become part of what makes people interesting and distinct, rather than being a trigger for fear and rejection. This movement happens most easily through personal encounters between particular people, which in turn transform many assistants' moral imagination at a more general level. Vanier's reflections underscore the power of two hearts meeting: L'Arche is about "changing the world one heart at a time." Another renowned Canadian philosopher, Charles Taylor, has argued that genuine compassion is always forged in the particulars (Taylor 1994).

Rabbi Jonathan Sacks's reflections on unity and peace echo their emphasis: "There is no road to general human solidarity that does not begin with moral particularity and loving specific human beings. . . . [T]here is no short-cut" (Sacks 2003, 58).

The problem is that some people never get the chance to experience these personal connections because their misunderstanding or inability to relate to people with disabilities closes them off from the start: they shrink shyly away from the chance, not knowing what to say or do. This is the missed opportunity that interests me. What stories could be shared that might invite nondisabled people's interest in being more open to what might unfold in such a connection? Attention to changing attitudes could be an important complement to legislation and rights.

To account for my assumption regarding the cultural background of discrimination and the isolation of people with disabilities, I briefly discuss how disability has been constructed as a deficit and how enhancing resources for people's moral imaginations can counter this. I then outline my primary research on the cultural milieu and enculturation processes of L'Arche, and I close by describing some of the lessons that the assistants commonly seem to learn from sharing their lives with people with developmental disability.

Disability as Deficit

It has been well established in disability studies that the category "developmental disability" derives as much from cultural constructions and social interactions as from biological realities (Roeher Institute 1996; Albrecht et al. 2001).[1] Some, especially in the United Kingdom, go so far as to dismiss the relevance of the biological reality altogether (Oliver 1990). How Western societies conceptualize people with developmental disabilities has been contingent on historical shifts in medical knowledge, as well as on economic and other factors. They have been characterized at different times as holy innocents or soulless beings, as blissfully happy or unpredictably violent (Wolfensberger 1973; Reinders, the introductory chapter above), as worthy of state protection and support or as those society needs protection from (Trent 1994; Stiker 1999a). A common representational thread is how

---

1. For definitions, see Fujiura (2005). This term is akin to "learning disability" in the U.K. and "mental retardation" in the U.S.

people with developmental disabilities are positioned as "the other" by people putting in the foreground what is uncommon about them rather than emphasizing what we share as humans (Davis 1997; Thomson 1996).

An extensive content analysis of media coverage for a contemporary disability-related murder case suggests that little has changed (Enns, 1999). Their unusual traits have almost always been considered undesirable, leading to a general image of them as devalued or deviant people whose very existence seems to contravene cultural norms and attract social controls (Goffman 1963; Roeher Institute 1996; Vanier 1989). Negative evaluations of impairment, storied abuses from the institutional era, and now genetic screening for fetal anomalies — all of these trace a repeated failure of our imagination. As a society we could not seem to imagine them as commensurate with ourselves.

Negative cultural representations of people with developmental disabilities continue in contemporary times. Critical analysis shows that even well-intentioned social scientists have tended to use the negatively slanted theories of stigma, labeling theory and deviance to interpret the role of impairment rather than looking through other possible lenses, such as liminality or pluralism (Klotz 2004; Murphy 1990; Shakespeare 1994). Medical professionals and geneticists generally persist in their focus on "deficit," which tends toward interventionist, individualized solutions that do not challenge the disabling social context (Davis 1997). The medical approach has, in fairness, developed life-enhancing treatments and technologies (see Newell, chap. 13 below). However, the issue is that their perspective dominates all others rather than working in concert with them, partly due to the medical professionals' central role as gatekeepers to resources such as funding through diagnoses that are by definition focused on areas of incompetence, not abilities.

The ongoing debates in moral philosophy and theology over whether and how concepts of personhood, suffering, justice, and spiritual capacity apply to people with developmental disabilities demonstrate that, for some, the status of their humanness remains contested.[2] Two phenomena underscore this persistent negative cultural outlook on disability: social exclusion and selective abortion. In spite of deinstitutionalization and over three decades of community living, the physical presence of people with developmental disabilities in urban settings remains grounded in a highly

2. For discussions of these issues, see Swinton 2001; Hauerwas 1986; Kittay 1999; and Reinders 2000.

circumscribed form of inclusion or tolerance (Stiker 1999a; Cushing 2003b; Bogdan and Taylor 1992). This is especially evident in the fact of their impoverished social networks (Lutfiya 1993; Brown et al. 1997; O'Brien and O'Brien 1993). Negativity is also evident in the virtually un-regulated and rapid rise of neo-eugenic uses of reproductive technologies[3] to "prevent" new babies with disabilities (Rapp and Ginsburg 2001; Asch 2001). Both issues pose serious questions about whether key legal and con-tractual gains made by disability rights advocates can actually change the hearts of the public (Reinders 2000). The potential for people with devel-opmental disabilities to make a positive contribution through their pres-ence remains misunderstood and undervalued by the public.

Disability and the Moral Imagination

I want to highlight the role imagination can play in shaping our actions. Coleridge helpfully distinguished between imagination as idle fancy and imagination that had the "shaping power to enable new reality to come into being" (Blackburn 1996). Critical theorists and liberation theologians have similarly considered the power of *conscientizacao* to illuminate the sociological and moral imagination of oppressed people and to inspire ac-tion against structural injustice (Freire 1985; Rivage-Seul 1994; Hinkelam-mert 1984). That formulation fits well with the social model of disability. Ethnographic theories of violence argue that imagination must precede action: actors first imagine what they will do and why, in order to legiti-mate and plan their acts (Schmidt and Schroeder 2001). Not surprisingly, parents report deep moral and religious reflection to clarify their beliefs and the outcomes in their imaginations prior to deciding whether to act on amniocentesis results (Rapp and Ginsburg 2001).

Blackburn defines imagination as "the ability to create and rehearse possible situations . . . and different approaches to a problem" (Blackburn 1996), implying some eventual action. Imagination is thus part of our pro-cess of world-making, and it mediates between goals, actions, and mean-ings. Reinders writes that liberal society cannot protect future children with developmental disabilities from emerging medical interventions that are aimed at preventing their birth without relying on nonliberal moral or

---

3. I use *neo-* here because parents technically "choose" abortion rather than its being state policy.

religious frameworks (Reinders 2000). I would add that there are not enough disability-positive cultural narratives in play for the nondisabled public to easily imagine a framework necessary to appreciate the value of a disabled presence. People who have few affirmative lenses through which to imagine or act also likely have little incentive to engage with people with disabilities in public settings, much less be prepared to welcome them into their families upon prenatal diagnosis.

The imagination is endowed through examples as well as lenses. Imagination is not merely made-up fiction; it is rooted in our life experiences. Imagination draws on the landscape of our habits, awareness, and relationships — influenced by the things we learn, do, or undergo, and populated by the people we know. In the field of character development, applied philosophers developed a typology that delineates six steps in the moral imagination process that move from creative thinking about problems and goals to developing and assessing alternative strategies and planning how to realize a solution (Lipman et al. 1980, 172-73). Clearly, awareness of alternative interpretations enhances our capacity to imagine disability anew and ideally leads toward transformed practices. The L'Arche experience is illustrative here because people connected with their homes do get a chance to enact the alternatives they learn about. Life-sharing gives them ample exposure to people with disabilities and an opportunity to observe experienced others interact, make mistakes, and adjust accordingly (Reimer, chap. 5 above). But where does the general public get its stories for understanding disability?

The cultural pool of positive images or stories about how people with developmental disabilities can enrich the fabric of society is certainly growing, but it is still dishearteningly small. There is a mounting pandisability literature of first-person narratives or assisted personal storytelling both in formal publications and in an explosion of online disability forums and blogs, such as Disaboom.com: "Everyone has a story, and now there's a place to share them. Connect with members as diverse as you are." Other research suggests a rising tide of representation of people with disabilities in the media and films, where stereotypes are sometimes reproduced and sometimes challenged (Riley 2005). Stories about families have had ambiguous influence. Parent narratives such as those of Oë (1995/2001), Brown (2007), or Brock (chap. 10 below) have long been a source of rich and affirmative images (Jackson 2006; Landsman 1997) and even policy change (Panitch 2008). However, they have not generally caught the popular imagination in a pervasive way; perhaps they are less persuasive for readers without a kin connection to disability. In addition, even those endorsements are often obscured by increasing numbers of reports on the increase in family stress and costs that a disabled child occasions, including higher risks of marital instability (Zajczyk 1995, 93-94) and social exclusion (Paughm 1995, 50). The general public has a limited pool of positive stories or experiences to draw on to fund their imaginations.

That dearth has performative consequences: many disability biographies and research reports detail how the difference of disability tends to occasion an interpersonal awkwardness and tension that diminishes the likelihood that "natural" acceptance or engagement will unfold, especially with new people (Amado 1993; Barton 1989). An American professor whose cognitive impairment occurred mid-career has written candidly about how even old friends shrank from him in embarrassed discomfort (Murphy 1990, 86). Indeed, Makas creatively taps into research on the efficacy of earlier U.S. racial integration efforts that were premised on the "contact hypothesis": that is, more interracial contact will reduce negative attitudes. The literature review demonstrates the importance of the extent and quality of the contact. The hypothesis holds only when the contact is significant and positive (Makas 1993, 128-33), and apparently this is not often the case. Fully 58 percent of nondisabled Americans said they are "often" or "occasionally" "awkward or embarrassed" when encountering people with disabilities; 47 percent experienced "fear"; while 74 percent felt "pity" (Harris 1991, cited in Makas 1993, 126).

This resistance to difference is not surprising if we consider disability as a form of cultural difference, as many in the disability movement do. Anthropologists have shown that ethnocentrism is a kind of universal human default setting that provides protection and identity functions, but that can close us off to fruitful new relationships if it is not tempered with compassion (Geertz 1994; Levi-Strauss 1985). Appreciating and welcoming people who are different from us is neither natural nor easy for humans to achieve. The other's differences challenge parts of our worldview and create uncertainty in us (Geertz 1994), which is uncomfortable and creates interaction strain. The problem of the stranger and our tendency to "dislike the unlike" is a most vexing moral and spiritual issue (Sacks 2003, 58-59), all the more so for people whose differences we do not value. But parochialism is not impervious to change; the point is that we should not underestimate the challenge. Although mere exposure is not enough to improve attitudes toward those of a different race or those differently abled — and can even worsen them if the exposure is negative — attitudes are somewhat malleable. Makas's literature review enumerates several qualitative and quantitative factors in contact moments that are proven to heighten the likelihood of attitude transformation (Makas 1993, 132).

Indeed, while contact does not always lead to relationships or transformed attitudes, there are certainly examples of when this does happen, that is, when fruitful, mutual nonkinship relationships thrive across disability in spite of various challenges (Lutfiya 1993; O'Brien and O'Brien 1993). More than twenty-five years ago, Stanley Hauerwas wrote about the hopefulness of these relationships: people with developmental disabilities call us to form a society that believes our differences help each of us to flourish (Hauerwas 1982, 64 [paraphrased]). In the remainder of this paper, I will discuss one community organization that has developed into an example and symbol of the human enjoyment and enrichment that are possible in and through such relationships.

The Cultural Milieu of L'Arche

An emergent theme in disability studies literature calls for the development of a more pluralistic framework for social inclusion of people with disability that is reminiscent of the push for multiculturalism. In a pluralist approach, the *alterity* of disability is not devalued, glossed over, or ignored; instead, it is given consideration as significant to what people contribute to the social fabric with and through their alterity — not in spite of it. Stiker contrasts this with other less fundamental forms of inclusion that he argues really only lead to indifference, inequality, or denial (Stiker 1999b; see also Devlieger et al. 2003).

For instance, as progressive as normalization and disability rights theories have been, both stake their demand for respect mainly on the fact that people are on a continuum of normalcy or simply because they are human (that is, in spite of abnormalities). Neither offers caregivers or the public the vital rationale needed to inspire a change in attitude that moves toward the acceptance of people with disabilities as they are: *with* their differences, not *in spite of* them.[4] Regarding their findings about the negative assumptions about children with impairments, Rapp and Ginsburg write about a desirable future "cultural terrain in which disability is not just begrudgingly accommodated . . . but is positively incorporated into the social

---

4. See also Sacks (2003, 56); Taylor and Bogdan (1989); and Reinders (2000).

body" (Rapp and Ginsburg 2001, 535). Such terrains do exist in small pockets: the international Camphill communities and schools, for instance, are built around precisely this idea (Jackson 2006). L'Arche is another example of such a site.

From a process standpoint, my research explored what kind of cultural milieu can reverse the usual Western indifference to or devaluation of people with intellectual disabilities. Literary historians have demonstrated that our experience is not raw, or "natural"; it is culturally mediated and is thus already an interpretation (Scott 1992, 37). If caregivers spend time with people with developmental disabilities without instruction in alternative lenses, the risk is that their prior negative or ambivalent conceptions can be reproduced in the new experiences (Makas 1993, 129). Instead, L'Arche has created a mediating subcultural milieu that effectively enculturates new assistants, facilitating their ability to interpret their experiences differently and contribute to the mission. Interestingly, though it is a faith-based community, my demographic and motivation profiles of Canadian assistants revealed that "disability" and "faith" were less important reasons to live there than their desire to "make a difference" or have an "experience of difference" (Cushing 2003a).[5] This means that for close to a majority of Canadian assistants, even the theological basis for the L'Arche philosophy must be learned. In keeping with Jean Vanier's nondogmatic approach, this cultural milieu has principles and structures, but it also gives wide room for assistants' agency: ultimately, each person chooses how to interpret these principles in particular relationships and how she or he will embody them in practice.

There are three elements that work in tandem to constellate the preconditions for a transformed caregiver subjectivity: life-sharing with people with developmental disabilities (in all their diversity); the example of experienced assistants; and the organizational culture or ethos, which includes spirituality.[6] From the outset, Vanier adhered to the gospel prescription to live closely with the poor, as he was mentored by a prophetic Dominican, Fr. Phillipe Thomas, to be radically present with the men in the asylum. Eventually they became the cofounders of L'Arche (Vanier, chap. 1 above). Vanier has consistently said, however, that it was primarily through *life-sharing* that the gospel ideas made deep sense to him and be-

---

5. Spiritual elements ranked higher for people once they had lived in the L'Arche community, and in the reasons they gave to *stay*.

6. *Ethos* is a social group's moral and aesthetic tone (Geertz 1973, 89).

came fully integrated in his work (Vanier, 1981). Just as Aristotle considered life-sharing to be fundamental to genuine *philia,* Vanier felt that this was central to his unfolding relationships of mutuality.

The people with disabilities (called "core members" of L'Arche) are the defining influence on the ethos and life of L'Arche: how they live in the world provides a daily example of the virtues of human variation, and it often offers insightful life lessons to the assistants. Nils Christie is eloquent on the influential role of "extraordinary people" (with impairments) in sustaining the vitality in the social life of Camphill communities: "They are themselves in most situations partly because some of them do not have the ability to pretend to be other than they are in private — they are the same in all conditions" (quoted in Cayley 1996, 23). They are an abiding source of inspiration, and they act as a touchstone for L'Arche assistants to remind them of what is important in life and in the mission.[7] Experienced assistants are also models for new caregivers — something akin to what Reimer calls moral exemplars (chap. 5 above) — though they would be the first to indicate that this should not imply any perfection on their part. The often transformative learning that assistants experience in L'Arche is jointly enabled through the community's philosophical anthropology and how that is shared by experienced assistants through modeling and storytelling.[8] In other words, people learn *how* to learn from and with the core members through these mechanisms. So these elements are interwoven and mutually informing.

How to embody this philosophy is neither natural nor self-evident to new people. L'Arche assistants in Canada learn how to be open to people with disabilities as they are in two main ways: in formal training and retreats and through experiential learning in everyday life. The cultural ethos is highly compelling but general, and by its nature it is something of a regulative ideal. Its countercultural character, however, means it can be difficult for assistants to fully internalize and apply the general principles in particular

---

7. One colorful and historical Canadian example of the symbolic power of developmental disability is found in novelist Robertson Davies's description of the influence his profoundly disabled brother had on the protagonist's character-building through holding commonality and difference in tension. "Ah, for Francis [his brother] was a lifelong reminder of the inadmissible primitive . . . a lifelong adjuration to pity, a sign that disorder and abjection stand less than a hair's breadth away from every human creature . . . a constant pointer to humility" (1985, 215).

8. My research supports Reimer's argument (chap. 5 above) that much of the assistants' moral functioning could be characterized as eventually taking on an "automaticity," or a sense of habituation.

situations. Experienced assistants and spiritual accompaniers help here, because they embody the philosophy in personalized ways. This cultural translation helps new assistants become familiar with the L'Arche approach, and eventually helps them learn and grow directly from people with disabilities.

It is significant that assistants develop their cultural fluency in actual daily practices and relationships. These practices are imbued with the significance of "ultimate contexts" by the L'Arche philosophy and theology. It is worth noting that assistants interpret "ultimate context" diversely: while there is broad consensus on the project of solidarity with those who are rejected, assistants' characterizations of the meaning of this project blend humanist and theological elements quite freely. The primacy of action in the development of habits of peace is discussed in this book by Vanier (chap. 1 above) and Hauerwas (chap. 9 below). Building on their insights, I underscore that the actions assistants undertake in L'Arche, and the meaning they make of them, they learn from people with disabilities within a specific cultural context, and those actions are not, on the whole, merely natural or inevitable outcomes of simple contact. Interviews and ethnographic observation all suggest a clear link between the enrichment of assistants' imaginations and the scope of actions they could even envision. As Vanier himself has said, "It is not a question of doing extraordinary things, but rather of doing ordinary things with love" (Vanier 1998).

Assistants discuss how these transitions of their worldview are both exciting and taxing, and require time, space, and various supports. Through listening to and observing assistants, I discerned six additional elements of the enculturation process of L'Arche. Each element plays a role in enabling assistants to grow in readiness and ability to be open to authentic relationships with people with developmental disabilities and to the possibility of transformation through them. I will simply outline them here; but I have elaborated them elsewhere (Cushing 2003a), including how most are rooted in religious principles or Vanier's interpretations of the gospel. Note how several points link directly to the particular character of a community built with and around people with disabilities.

1. *Organization of space and time* reflects and reproduces L'Arche's cultural values and desired outcomes, especially as it privileges the central presence of core members.
2. *Informal storytelling among all members* is valued and used to indirectly communicate values and disability-positive lessons to assistants in everyday life.

3. *Redefining productivity as fecundity* challenges the limited definition of productivity as labor with the concepts of fecundity and generativity, which encompass alternative forms of value.

4. *Revalorizing devalued difference* is an attempt to promote a strong case for the social value of disability as illustrated by core members' influence on L'Arche.

5. *Solidarity and power rebalancing* switches the burden of change from people with disabilities to assistants, who learn to recognize the unconventional gifts of people with disabilities.

6. *Caring for the caregivers* is accomplished through various communal and individual mechanisms that support the caregivers to continue to serve well.

Common Changes in Assistants

Through fieldwork and ongoing collaboration with L'Arche in Canada and internationally for almost a decade, I have been humbled by the unpredictability and grace that characterizes the diverse ways that people are shaped and inspired by life-sharing with core members and others in the local moral world of L'Arche. There are numerous ways one could slice up this pie of common changes. I do not imagine that my breakdown is either definitive or exhaustive, but it is an attempt to corral these movements into some categories.

It is not by accident that most of the points do not seem major: big dramatic changes are neither common nor trusted in the grounded atmosphere of L'Arche homes. The routine structure of their daily life dictates against grand claims and instead encourages transformations that are small but sustainable — hard to live but directionally radical. Experienced assistants also emphasize that the character of this learning process is distinct. Clara explains: "Core members can be such good teachers partly because they are not trying to teach you. That opens you right up." Warren adds: "When assistants experience the radical acceptance they receive from core members, they let down their guard and are able to be open to what emerges in their relationships." Overall, it is my sense that the circumference of what the assistants are able to imagine as valuable or desirable expands as their capacity to be in front of — and to appreciate — devalued differences develops.

Presence

One of the simplest points I heard was also clearly profound for people. They spoke of a growing capacity and desire to be present to each moment they lived. Part of the challenge for people accustomed to the pace and expectations of the regular world is to learn the value in simply being present (see editor's introduction above). Many said that this contrasted with the norms they grew up with, where being busy and doing things are symbols of being an important person. Presence is also partly a challenge because it is bound up with the question of whether I will be valued and loved just as I am — if I am not "doing for." I recall an experienced assistant gently helping me to understand that there was no need for me to spend all afternoon making gourmet meals. She said that they would rather that I spend time relaxing with core members. The underlying message I heard — or perhaps needed to hear — was: "Don't worry, we'll still like you if you just make spaghetti."

Not all *presence* is created equal: physical presence does not guarantee quality of attention. Many assistants shared stories about learning what it means to be centered and how to retain or regain that balance during challenging times. The labor of care can be emotionally trying, so L'Arche provides guidance, especially through prayer retreats. Assistants are also encouraged to be self-reflective in order to better support core members. People do this in diverse ways: through prayer, through writing letters, rollerblading, or reading a book.

Patience

Parents in and outside of L'Arche often comment that with most people who have developmental disabilities, you have no choice but to move at their pace and on their timeline (Kittay 1999; Oë 2001; Brown 2007). If you remain in the mindset typical of our hurried, task-oriented society, this can be incredibly frustrating: the to-do list will become your cross to bear. Oë writes with characteristic honesty of hitting a low point when he became so annoyed with his son Hikari's dawdling in a store that he left to do his task. Upon his return, Hikari was missing, which triggered his shame and panic over his lack of patience. Oë dramatizes what every assistant or parent feels at some point — and perhaps feels often. This is part of why so many assistants make the cultivating of their own patience a priority. It's certainly possible that other assistants can try one's patience as well! Stanley Hauerwas's essay in this volume (chap. 9 below) insightfully connects this learning to being a peacemaker in the world. I think this dimension of patience is also related to learning to let go, that is, accepting that you cannot control many things. Assistants often confided to me that they had a strong desire to cultivate patience in order to accept what is given or unfolds on their unpredictable days.

Receptivity

In line with the gospel's valuing of the small and the weak, Vanier has always emphasized the importance of the small, simple things in life. People learn that the trivial daily habits that are not normally seen as significant or sources of pleasure are actually fundamental to one's happiness. Aristotle also felt that such daily intimacies were vital to developing *philia*. Attention to what is small and allegedly unremarkable seems to have the effect of cultivating receptivity in assistants who become more open and flexible to what emerges. They learn to be more open to learning from people with disabilities as they experience the insight, inspiration, humor, surprise, and sometimes dissonance of disability.

Jack, a core member who struggles with anxiety over routines, believes a good afternoon is relaxing on the couch with a coke with the time to talk himself through the events of his workday: who bothered him, what he ate, what was happening tomorrow, and so forth. I have seen him "train" many assistants in how to be more receptive during those moments: they see how he settles in and finds some relief in this ritual, and if you want to be part of his journey and understand him, you must be attentive and receptive to the subtle shifts of his mutterings and stories from day to day. Perhaps due to the distinct characters in L'Arche, it is also common to find a real receptivity in everyone to enjoy the unexpected or silly things in life.

Personal and Spiritual Authenticity

One of the most common areas of growth that people cited was their evolving willingness to bring their whole self into their relationships. Many noted that when they experienced the relief of being fully accepted by core members, they felt less need to be guarded about their own imperfection and fragility. They even had the desire to continue that personal authenticity in other relationships and settings. Many seem to realize subconsciously that no core member would be the same person without his or her particular brokenness. Therefore, it stands to reason that the assistants' own brokenness could be distinctly lovable, too. They came to recognize that we are constituted equally by our strengths and our weaknesses (Vanier, chap. 1 above). Spiritual authenticity is described most often as practicing or "living what I believe in." Fittingly, this is a common motive for coming to L'Arche. "I have spent so much time in school reading about how to be a good person," said one philosophy student. "Now I want to actually try to live it."

Other-orientation

The nature of the role is explicitly about supporting other people toward liberation, helping them to live their lives well, so this turn toward the other is a necessary transition. It is an especially marked lesson for today's young assistants, who have been called "Generation Me" and who often remark on the challenge of making the shift toward greater attentiveness to someone else's needs. Assistants learn about the rich possibilities in relationships on the continuum of mutuality rather than seeing care as a one-way, charitable act. Through these relationships they also develop an ability to recognize and appreciate the unconventional gifts that others have to share. Many spoke of how they have learned to be more generous with their spirit and time through seeing how core members give of themselves so freely. Many give back by going beyond the basic physics of care.

Finally, many people spoke about learning from core members to be more forgiving. This comes partly from experiencing the gift of forgiveness core members inadvertently bestow on you when they wake up and are no longer annoyed at you for yesterday's mistakes. It also comes from living with people who are not always capable of behaving differently, no matter how much *you* think it should be possible. Assistants see this learning as especially important since the intensity of life in the homes commonly produces conflicts of various kinds that need to be worked through.

Conclusion

When I say that the caregivers' moral imaginations are expanding, I mean that people appear to leave L'Arche with an imaginative toolbox that is larger and more versatile than when they arrived. I have tried to illustrate the cultural processes at work in L'Arche that help to facilitate the ability and willingness of caregivers there to learn from the people with disabilities. These lessons enhance their ability to be effective support-providers, but they also transform their moral imaginations in ways that transcend this local experience of disability and speak to their formation as everyday peacemakers in our world.

One challenge for L'Arche is how it might become a more recognizable symbol of the value of people with developmental disability, perhaps through developing better ways to disseminate the stories of what they live. Although there has been a clear liberalization in the attitudes of many practitioners and academics, anachronistic cultural scripts continue to pervade the public imagination and the popular portrayals of developmental disability. L'Arche has the cultural and narrative resources to help enlarge the pool of affirmative representations of life with disabilities and to stem the increasing prominence of medical and public scripts that seem to write them out of our world.

References

Albrecht, G. L., K. D. Seelman, and M. Bury, eds. 2001. *Handbook of disability studies.* Thousand Oaks, CA: Sage.

Amado, A. N., ed. 1993. *Friendships and community connections between people with and without intellectual disabilities.* Baltimore: Paul H. Brookes.

Asch, A. 2001. Disability, bioethics and human rights. In *Handbook of disability studies,* ed. G. L. Albrecht, K. D. Seelman, and M. Bury. Thousand Oaks, CA: Sage.

Barton, L. 1989. Integration: Myth or reality? In *Integration: Myth or reality?* ed. L. Barton, 1-5. London: Falmer Press.

Blackburn, S. 1996. Imagination. In *Oxford Dictionary of Philosophy,* 187. New York: Oxford University Press.

Bogdan, R., and S. J. Taylor. 1992. The social construction of humanness: Relationships with severely disabled people. In *Interpreting disability: A qualitative reader,* ed. P. Ferguson, D. Ferguson, and S. J. Taylor, 275-94. New York: Teachers College Press.

Brown, I. 2007. Finding Walker's place: The boy in the moon. *The Globe and Mail* [electronic version]: http://www.theglobeandmail.com/v5/content/features/focus/boyinthemoon (accessed Dec. 8, 2007).

Brown, I., D. Raphael, and R. Renwick, eds. 1997. *Quality of life — dream or reality? Life for people with developmental disabilities in Ontario.* Centre for Health Promotion, University of Toronto.

Cayley, D. 1994. *Beyond Institutions II.* Radio documentary. Toronto: Canadian Broadcasting Corporation (March).

Cushing, P. 2003a. *Shaping the moral imagination of caregivers: Disability, difference and inequality in L'Arche.* PhD diss., Hamilton, Ont.: McMaster University.

———. 2003b. *Report on social inclusion and exclusion policies.* Toronto: The Roeher Institute.

Davies, R. 1985. *What's bred in the bone.* Toronto: Penguin Books.

Davis, L. J. 1997. Constructing normalcy: The Bell Curve, the novel, and the invention of the disabled body in the nineteenth century. In *The disability studies reader,* ed. L. J. Davis, 9-28. New York: Routledge.

Devlieger, P., F. Rusch, and D. Pfeiffer. 2003. *Rethinking disability: The emergence of new definitions, concepts and communities.* Antwerp and Apeldoorn: Garant.

Enns, R. 1999. *A voice unheard: The Latimer case and people with disabilities.* Halifax, Nova Scotia: Fernwood Publishing.

Freire, P. 1985. *The politics of education: Culture, power and liberation.* Trans. D. Macedo. New York: Bergin and Garvey.

Fujuira, G. T. 2005. Developmental disabilities. In *Encyclopedia of disability,* ed. G. L. Albrecht, 1: 394-97. Thousand Oaks, CA: Sage.

Geertz, C. 1973. Religion as a cultural system. In *The interpretation of cultures,* 87-125. New York: Basic Books/HarperCollins.

———. 1994. The uses of diversity. In *Assessing cultural anthropology,* ed. R. Borofsky, 454-66. New York: McGraw-Hill.

Ginsburg, F., and R. Rapp. 1991. The politics of reproduction. *Annual Review of Anthropology* 20: 311-43.

Goffman, E. 1963. *Stigma: Notes on the management of spoiled identity.* Englewood Cliffs, NJ: Prentice Hall.

Hauerwas, S. 1986. *Suffering presence: Theological reflections on medicine, the mentally handicapped, and the church.* Notre Dame, IN: University of Notre Dame Press.

———, ed. 1982. *Responsibility for devalued persons: Ethical interactions between society, the family, and the retarded.* Springfield, MA: Charles C. Thomas.

Hinkelammert, F. 1984. *Critica a la razon utopica.* San Jose, Costa Rica: Dept. Ecumenico de Investigaciones.

Jackson, R. 2006. *Holistic special education: Camphill principles and practice.* Edinburgh: Floris Books.

———, ed. 1996. *Bound to care: An anthology.* Cheshire, UK: RESCARE.

Kittay, E. F. 1999. *Love's labor: Essays on women, equality, and dependency.* New York and London: Routledge.

Klotz, J. 2004. Socio-cultural study of intellectual disability: Moving beyond labeling and social constructionist perspectives. *British Journal of Learning Disabilities* 34: 93-104.

Landsman, G. 1997. Concepts of personhood and mothers of persons with disabilities. *Disability Studies Quarterly* 17: 157-76.

Levi-Strauss, C. 1985. *The view from afar.* New York: Basic Books.

Lipman, M., A. Sharp, and F. Oscanyan. 1980. *Philosophy in the classroom* (2nd ed.). Philadelphia: Temple University Press.

Louis Harris and Associates, Inc. 1991. *Public attitudes toward people with disabilities.* Study No. 912028. Washington, DC: National Organization on Disability.

Lunsky, Y. 2002. Psychosocial risk factors for mental health problems in adults with developmental disabilities. Conference paper. Richmond Hill, Ont.: Ontario Association for Developmental Disabilities.

Lutfiya, Z. M. 1993. When "staff" and "clients" become friends. In *Friendships and community connections between people with and without intellectual disabilities,* ed. A. N. Amado, 97-108. Baltimore: Paul H. Brookes.

Makas, E. 1993. Getting in touch: The relationship between contact with, and attitudes towards people with disabilities. In *Perspectives on Disability* (2nd ed.), ed. M. Nagler, 121-36. Palto Alto, CA: Health Markets Research.

Murphy, R. 1990. *The body silent.* New York: W. W. Norton.

O'Brien, J., and C. L. O'Brien. 1993. Unlikely alliances: Friendships and people with developmental disabilities. In *Friendships and community connections between people with and without intellectual disabilities,* ed. A. N. Amado, 9-39. Baltimore, MD: Paul H. Brookes.

Oë, K. 1995/2001. *A healing family: A candid account of life with a disabled son.* New York: Kodansha Press.

Oliver, M. 1990. *The politics of disablement.* London: Macmillan.

Panitch, M. 2008. *Disability, mothers, and organization: Accidental activists.* New York: Routledge.

Paughm, S. 1995. The spiral of precariousness: A multidimensional approach to the process of social disqualification in France. In *Beyond the threshold,* ed. G. Room, 49-79. Bristol, UK: Policy Press.

Priestly, M. 2002. Why we need to work together in the European Year of Disabled People. *Disability and Society* 17 (7): 845-49.

Rapp, R., and F. Ginsburg. 2001. Enabling disability: Rewriting kinship, reimagining citizenship. *Public Culture* 13 (3): 533-56.

Reinders, H. S. 2000. *The future of the disabled in liberal society: An ethical analysis.* Notre Dame, IN: University of Notre Dame Press.

Riley, C. A. 2005. *Disability and the media: Prescriptions for change.* Hanover, NH: University Press of New England.

Rivage-Seul, M., and M. Rivage-Seul. 1994. Critical thought and moral imagination: Peace education in Freirean perspective. In *Politics of Liberation: Paths from Freire*, ed. P. L. McLaren and C. Lankshear, 41-61. London: Routledge.

Roeher Institute. 1996. *Disability, community and society: Exploring the links.* Toronto: The Roeher Institute.

Sacks, J. 2003 [2002]. *The dignity of difference: How to avoid the clash of civilizations.* London: Continuum.

Schmidt, B. E., and I. Schroeder, eds. 2001. *Anthropology of violence and conflict.* London: Routledge.

Scott, J. W. 1992. Experience. In *Feminists theorize the political,* ed. J. Butler and J. W. Scott, 22-40. New York: Routledge.

Shakespeare, T. 1994. Cultural representation of disabled people: Dustbins for disavowal? *Disability and Society* 9 (3): 283-99.

Stiker, H.-J. 1999a [1997]. *A history of disability.* Trans. W. Sayers. Ann Arbor: University of Michigan Press.

———. 1999b. Using historical anthropology to think disability. In *Disability in Different Cultures: Reflections on local concepts,* ed. B. Holzer, A. Vreede, and G. Weigt, 352-80. Piscataway, NJ: Transaction.

Swinton, J. 2001. Spirituality and the lives of people with learning disabilities. *Updates* 3 (6): 1-4.

Taylor, C. 1994. Philosophical reflections on caring practices. In *The crisis of care,* ed. S. S. Phillips and P. E. Benner, 174-88. Washington: Georgetown University Press.

Taylor, S. J., and R. Bogdan. 1989. On accepting relationships between people with mental retardation and non-disabled people: Towards an understanding of acceptance. *Disability, Handicap and Society* 4 (1): 21-36.

Thomson, R. G., ed. 1996. *Freakery: Cultural spectacles of the extraordinary body.* New York: New York University Press.

Trent, J. W. 1994. *Inventing the feeble mind: A history of mental retardation in the United States* (vol. 6). Berkeley and Los Angeles: University of California Press.

Vanier, J. 1981. *The challenge of L'Arche.* Ottawa: Novalis.

———. 1989. *Community and growth.* Trans. J. Vanier (2nd rev. ed.). New York: Paulist Press.

———. 1998. *Becoming human.* Toronto: Anansi.

Wolfensberger, W., ed. 1973. *A selective overview of the work of Jean Vanier and the movement of L'Arche.* Toronto: National Institute on Mental Retardation (Roeher).

Zajczyk, F. 1995. Between survey and social services analysis: An inquiry 'On two lines and three levels.' In *Beyond the threshold,* ed. G. Room, 80-101. Bristol, UK: Policy Press.

Chapter Seven

The Sign of Contradiction

XAVIER LE PICHON

Jesus Christ as a Sign of Contradiction

I borrow this title from a retreat preached by Cardinal Wojtyla, the future Pope John Paul II, in 1976 to the then pope Paul VI and his collaborators. Wojtyla commented on the words of the old man Simeon to Mary, as she came with Joseph to the temple in Jerusalem for the presentation of their forty-day-old infant Jesus, according to the Gospel of Luke:

> And Simeon blessed them, and said unto Mary his mother, "Behold, this child is set for the fall and rising again of many in Israel; and for a sign which shall be spoken against; (Yea, a sword shall pierce through thy own soul also,) that the thoughts of many hearts may be revealed (Luke 2:34-35, KJV). (Cardinal Wojtyla 1979)

Instead of the King James translation of the Greek words *semeion antilegomenon* ("a sign which shall be spoken against"), Wojtyla uses "a sign of contradiction," which I find quite helpful in getting into a deeper understanding of these extraordinary words. It is my hope to use these words to enlighten my vision of the place persons with disabilities have progressively taken into my life as I entered with my family into a new friendship with them, friendship that has thoroughly changed our life. Yes, the people I met every day in L'Arche more than thirty years ago have been a sign of contradiction for me, which has revealed many thoughts that I did not even know to be present in myself. I believe that what is true of me has also been true for the whole of humanity ever since men and women first confronted themselves with the significance of life they were discovering. I believe that it is one of the main challenges confronting our world today.

The lecture on the Gospels that Wojtyla made during this retreat is one in which he presents Jesus to the reader as this sign of contradiction who revealed to us the mystery of our human nature made in the image of God, but which is fragile and vulnerable, an image of God hidden within a "vessel made of clay" (Jer. 18:6). The Gospels demonstrate that Jesus was this sign of contradiction all the way from his infancy to his death on the cross. At the beginning of his earthly existence, the powerless baby as an incarnation of the Son of God is a first obvious sign of contradiction. Why does the all-powerful God choose to adopt the life of a baby craving for the love of his mother? At the end of his life, the horrible death on the cross, "stumbling block for the Jews and foolishness for the Greeks" (1 Cor. 1:23) is the second very striking sign of contradiction. The Gospel of John shows Jesus being presented by Pilate to the crowd as "the human" (*ho anthropos*: "Behold the man," John 19:5) at the time when Jesus is suffering, scorned, and humiliated. Man in his suffering, man wounded and tortured, at this moment in history more than any other, reveals the mystery of his humanity, in which the image of God is hidden. From the beginning of early Christianity, Jesus' disciples identified him with the "suffering servant" of Isaiah: "As many were astonished at thee; his visage was so marred more than any man, and his form more than the sons of men" (Isa. 52:14).

But we should never forget that Jesus first chose to reveal himself as a baby. Thus Jesus chose to reveal his humanity to us as both the innocent infant and the "suffering servant" and in this way to reveal our deepest thoughts as we are confronted by this double sign of contradiction related to our birth and our death.

The Two Golden Ages of Humans

In the Gospels, Jesus as an infant, Jesus as a man entering into his agony provokes us so that we may search within our deepest thoughts for who we are. Indeed, there is a mystery in the infant, there is a mystery in the old age and the agony to which it leads. Fr. Thomas Philippe, the cofounder of L'Arche with Jean Vanier, considered the infancy and the old age with its proximity of death and its suffering as the two golden ages of humans, the ages during which the Holy Spirit can act in a very special way because of the immense love of God for those who are craving for love and suffer so much because they do not receive the tenderness for which they are desperate. And what Father Thomas discovered here, during the thirty years he spent with disabled men and women in L'Arche, is that these men and women belong to both ages. They have the innocence of infants but the sufferings of aged persons. As a result, they have the special gifts that accompany both ages, gifts that one can only discover when one enters into a deep personal relationship with these people with disabilities, gifts that are indissolubly tied to their vulnerability.

Of course, to discover the gifts that bless these two ages, one should not consider infants simply as future adults, and old men and women at the end of their lives simply as former adults, which our society tends more and more to do. We have to consider them as infants and as humans at the end of their lives, humans who are able to love and thus have the full dignity of humans, and who are entitled to be treated as free persons, because love cannot exist without freedom and dignity. This is, of course, also true for persons with disabilities. When the disabilities are permanent, we cannot consider those persons independently of their disabilities. It is so deeply rooted in them that any attempt to treat them as if they were not disabled is bound to fail. This is the limit of so-called normalization attempts. I have always been impressed by the fact that in Luke (24:39) and John (20: 20-27), Jesus identifies himself after his resurrection by showing the scars left by the nails and the spear. For Luke and John, resurrection did not obliterate the marks of his crucifixion but sublimated them. The sacrifice of the cross, for Luke and John, is now part of the identity of Jesus. Such a suffering experience cannot be detached from the person; it becomes part of the person's identity.

An infant, a person of old age, a person with disabilities whatever the age — all have their own identity. It is only when we come into contact with their identity that they can not only touch our hearts but can deeply transform us, our society. This will happen in the measure that we agree to enter into a humble relationship based on respect, love, and a search for understanding, for discovery of their own dignity, their own freedom, in the measure in which we believe that we have something crucial to learn from them about themselves as well as about ourselves. In other words, each age of life, each human condition, has its unique value, its unique gifts. The more hidden they are, the more important they become for us once they have been discovered. This is the essence of our humanity.

The Denial of Our Vulnerability in Contemporary Society

A common characteristic of infants, persons of great age, and persons with disabilities is their vulnerability. But our society is less and less able to cope with vulnerable persons. In our society, vulnerability is a flaw, a shortcoming that one should try to eliminate. Our society finds no value in vulnerability. This is paradoxical in my view, because I believe that the discovery of the vulnerability of our prehuman ancestors has played a decisive role in the process of humanization (Le Pichon 1997). Indeed, our society is more or less consciously trying to eliminate the signs of contradiction that appear through the diverse manifestations of our vulnerability.

As an example of this, let me quote here a letter just published in the French newspaper *Le Monde* on February 8, 2007. The author of the letter, Nicolas Journet, is a scenarist affected by Marfan syndrome. In his letter Journet comments on the French parliamentary debates about the revision of the law on bioethics. "Today, they consider making the prenatal diagnostic obligatory for this disease, *my* disease" (italics added). The debates claimed that this measure would enable physicians to follow infants with Marfan syndrome from their birth. "Provided one allows them to be born," comments Nicolas Journet. "Who will explain to the parents that genetic disease and happiness are not antinomic terms?" From the diagnosis of his disease, during his adolescence, "under the eyes of powerless parents who asked themselves how they could have engendered such a sum of imperfections," until he was able to live with his disease and find his place in society, Nicolas Journet has known "the shame . . . the escape within myself." Yet he claims that he now feels that he is "very happy," "much happier than many genetically correct people." Nicolas Journet believes that the will to generalize the prenatal diagnosis shows that our society "does not want to face death, does not want to leave place to any hazard."

I do not wish to consider here the very complex problem of the double message that our society sends to genetically affected people by caring for them while trying to eliminate genetically affected fetuses before they are born (Reinders 2000). Rather, I want to point out that Nicolas Journet speaks about his genetic disease as "mine." It is his disease — a part of himself — and he learned, indeed, how to live once he accepted that the Marfan syndrome was part of himself. In my opinion, he has correctly diagnosed that the "sign of contradiction" related to his identity as a genetically diseased person, the sign of contradiction that he had to face all his life, and first in his relationship with his parents, was in great part related to the fact that our society does not want to face death. I would add that our society does not want to face suffering, and does not want to face vulnerability in general.

Recognizing Vulnerability as Part of Human Understanding since the Origin of Our Species

I continue to argue that trying to eliminate these signs of contradiction is a dangerous new path for humanity. This is clear once we pay attention to the recent findings of paleoanthropologists. They show that, from the early beginnings of our humanity, our ancestors understood that vulnerability is at the essence of what it is to be human. Consider, for example, the 100,000-year-old Shanidar 1 skeleton. This skeleton belonged to a Neanderthal man who was about forty years old; he was discovered by Ralph Solecki during the 1950s in a cave in the Zagros mountains in Iraq (Trinkaus and Shipman 1993). This man was so severely handicapped that he could not have lived to his estimated age without the support of the group to which he belonged. According to Jane M. Renfrew, "he had suffered from a withered arm and shoulder probably from birth; his right ankle showed extensive arthritic degeneration; and he had received a severe blow to the left side of his face which was not fatal but would certainly have blinded his left eye" (Renfrew, in press).

When Solecki popularized his findings in a book entitled *The Flower People* (so named because the skeletons discovered in the Shanidar cave appear to have been buried beneath a bed of flowers), many scientists expressed strong doubts about his conclusions (Solecki 1971). Since then, it has been well established that Shanidar 1 was not an exception and that Neanderthalers "fed and looked after severely handicapped members of their communities who were too disabled to contribute to the food quest" (Trinkaus and Shipman 1993). Actually, the skepticism of the scientists appears to me to be another demonstration of how difficult it is for us to face this sign of contradiction, which certainly does not appear to fit straightforward Darwinian theory. Why did a small group of nomads, having to seek food by hunting and plant gathering every day, decide to radically reorganize their life so that a severely handicapped man would become the center of their efforts and attention? What did they receive from him to continue doing this for forty years? Why did they decide to bury him at a time when burial was reserved for only a few individuals? The latter fact was pointed out to me by my colleague at the Collège de France, the paleoanthropologist Yves Coppens. What did they discover about their own humanity through this long and arduous process of sharing their life with a severely disabled man? Was this their way of facing death and suffering?

The Shanidar 1 individual demonstrates to me that this sign of contradiction is at the very heart of our identity as humans since our origins. Actually, I have argued elsewhere that when humans, confronted with this sign of contradiction, enter into the kind of relationship that was lived within the Shanidar group of Neanderthals, the gift they receive from each other is the discovery of their own humanity (Le Pichon 1997). Our humanity is not an attribute that we have received once and forever at the time of our conception. It is a potentiality that we have to discover within us and progressively develop or destroy through our confrontation with the different signs of contradiction that we will encounter throughout our lives.

Vulnerability at the Core of the Exchange of Love through Communion

But what actually does happen within this relationship? How do we make this exchange of gifts? Fr. Thomas Philippe thought that everything came from our need for communion. He believed that our inner being — what he called our heart — can only grow when it is nurtured by love through this communion, which can mysteriously unite two human beings in the mutual sharing and treasuring of their presence. This heart, given to us as a capacity, progressively develops as it is filled by the memories of these instances of communion. But there is a memory of the heart that also registers the wounds that are inflicted when one is starved of communion. We can perhaps better feel what Fr. Philippe meant by the word of communion through the Gospel of John with the importance that is given to the concept of *menein* ("to dwell"): "The father who dwells in me" (John 14:10). "Rabbi, where do you dwell?" (John 1:38). It is this feeling that we can dwell in the other: his dwelling is our dwelling. We belong. We have complete confidence. The extraordinary thing is that this communion can occur between two human beings, whoever they are — infants, aged people, disabled ones, adults. And the experience of Fr. Philippe was that communion was often within easier reach of those who would be considered least developed by our society and least adapted to its demands. Through communion we actually make ourselves vulnerable to the other. Vulnerability becomes a common ground between the two persons entering into communion.

If this is so, then we understand why human beings are so fragile and vulnerable. Actually, fragility and vulnerability are the two essential components of humanity. We would not be what we are without this fragility and vulnerability. I have pleaded with a friend, Dominique Lambert, a professor of philosophy and physics at the University of Namur, for a scientific research program that seeks to consider the importance of the fragility and vulnerability of humans in the development of humanity. As I have implied in this short essay, I believe that vulnerability and fragility played an essential role in the origin and development of humanity. I also believe that the implicit and sometimes explicit denial of this fragility and vulnerability in our modern societies puts us in great danger of losing the meaning and value of human life. And there again we are at the heart of this "sign of contradiction," which forces us to make a choice between the richness of life, with its fragility and vulnerability, and the impoverishment and hardening of our societies.

References

Le Pichon, X. 1997. *Aux racines de l'homme, de la mort à l'amour.* Paris: Presses de la Renaissance.

Reinders, H. S. 2000. *The future of the disabled in liberal society: An ethical analysis.* Notre Dame: The University of Notre Dame Press.

Renfrew, J. (in press) Neanderthal symbolic behavior? In *Becoming human: Innovation in prehistoric material and spiritual culture,* ed. C. Renfrew and I. Morley. Cambridge: Cambridge University Press.

Solecki, R. 1971. *Shanidar: The first flower people.* New York: Knopf.

Trinkaus, E., and P. Shipman. 1993. *The Neanderthals: Changing the image of mankind.* New York: Alfred Knopf.

Wojtyla, C. 1979. *Le signe de contradiction.* Paris: Communio-Fayard.

PART IV

Responses from Theology

Chapter Eight

Learning from People with Disabilities:
How to Ask the Right Questions

WILLIAM C. GAVENTA

What Do We Learn from People with Disabilities?

When I served directly as chaplain in two large residential facilities earlier in my career, it became increasingly clear that there were two theological linchpins to everything I did: celebration and belonging. How could I and the seminarians who worked with me help people with severe disabilities, on the one hand, feel their gifts and value, and on the other, feel and be connected with others beyond those paid to be caregivers. Those were two ways of addressing the questions "Who am I?" and "Whose am I?" In this essay I will organize my reflections on what we learn from people with disabilities concerning these two questions. My aim is to show how the experience of actually engaging with people with disabilities changes our interest in the profound questions of what it means to be human and moves us to ask how we think about and shape our own identities in relationship — in community — with others.

Personhood and Identity

First, *who* are we? The question is about identity, but it has two sides. The questions initially posed when one enters into relationships with people with disabilities (for whatever reason) are usually not about *who* but *what*. What does it mean to be human? What does it mean to be disabled? Is there such a thing as "the disabled" or "the normal"? These are questions about adjectives, characteristics, and qualities that usually come with specific tasks. Many in the role of either direct caregivers, volunteers, fellow congregational members, or professional staff have told me about their beginning relationships with people with developmental disabilities on the basis of these people's labels and needs. After a while the labels and characterizations as "other" begin to fade into the background as individuals become known by their names, their unique personalities, their individual gifts, and their individual needs. Consequently, when people move into relationships with people with disabilities, the supposed distinctions begin to lose their significance. As Fr. John Aurelio, an author and fellow New York State institutional chaplain, once told me, people move from "fear" to "pity" to "anger" to "love." Fear of "the disabled" moves to "feeling sorry for," then to anger when one gets to know individuals and recognizes the stigma, injustices, and social limitations that compound and sometimes cause them to wear their labels. But in anger we can still "do for" or "try to save or fix" another, until we realize that while we may be doing something for them, there is a real mutuality going on, in which they are doing something for us, and we can begin to call that friendship and love (Vanier, chap. 1 above).

The shifting interest in questions asked indicates that the initial question, "Who am I?" only gradually turns into a question of identity. Only when we enter into relationships with them do people with disabilities become individuals, and only then may we begin to see them as people who bear our fears about what it means to be vulnerable, fragile, finite, limited, weak, and mortal. It fascinates me that when we talk about figures of power or prestige and get a revelation of one or more of those qualities in them, we talk about seeing their "human side." A politician cries in public, and he or she is either admired or denigrated for doing so. Actors come clean about their problems with addiction and their resolve to get help, and we then admire them even more, or we see in their "failings" our own. *Time* magazine runs a story about the dark night of the soul where Mother Teresa so often walked, and suddenly this saint becomes very, very human. Part of my fascination comes from the assumptions that success, fame, and power are predicated on perfection, control, or other superhuman qualities. Thus, getting to know people with disabilities as individual human beings raises a question regarding our own identity as humans: How do we learn to accept all about humanity that is fragile, vulnerable, and broken (see Le Pichon, preceding chap.)? Jürgen Moltmann said it in an essay about theology and disability:

In actual fact the distinction between the healthy and the handicapped does not exist. For every human life is limited, vulnerable, and weak. Helpless we are born and helpless we die. So in reality there is no such thing as a handicapped life. It is only the ideal of health set up by the society of the capable which condemns a certain group of people to be called "handicapped." (Moltmann 1983, 137)[1]

Questions such as what it means to be human, or what it is to be a person, can be used to identify characteristics and qualities that justify distinctions between people, that is, between "disabled" and "nondisabled" people. As such they are not very helpful. Early in my first job as the chaplain of a large state institution, long before I even knew I was doing something that others would later call qualitative research, I spent several weeks asking a number of my new congregants this question: What do you think it means to be a person? Two answers I never forgot were:

"I don't know, but I know it is the best thing you can be."
"I don't know, but God does, and he likes it."

If the distinction between "normal" and "disabled" becomes unintelligible or arbitrary, then the question of identity becomes more focused and challenging. Our call is not to identify ourselves by what we do not have, nor to identify others in that way. My question to the residents of that state school were partly prompted by my being horrified when one of the "higher-functioning" men came up to me one day and said, "Chaplain, you want to hear some moron jokes?" That was one of my first experiences of the ways in which people with disabilities participate in what is a far too "normal" activity of building our own identity and ego by putting others down. The Gospel of Luke has the story of Jesus telling a parable "to some who trusted in themselves that they were righteous and despised others" (Luke 18:9-14). There he points out that we are not to pray like the Pharisee, who says, "God, I thank you that I am not like other men" — that is, to claim our identity and worth by thanking the Lord we are not like those others.

Our challenge, then, is to claim who and what we are as humans, but to do so in a nonexclusive way. That task becomes one in which we become

---

1. To further Moltmann's point, the paradox is that we think we are anything else in between (Le Pichon, preceding chap.).

acutely aware of the power of words, as people search for the right labels or adjectives to define disability or shape public policy and response. Are you — am I — "disabled," or do I have a "disability"? This leads to further important questions: Who has the right to define who I am? How does any adjective, quality, or characteristic enter into our ways of defining persons, or a class of persons, thereby limiting our field of vision and what we see? In my personal experience, and in that of many others I count as colleagues and friends, one of the challenges we face is to first be honest about the ways we have received and learned from the very people we, as professionals who work in the field, have felt called or drawn to serve.

More simply put, one of the gifts to me and other caregivers has been the ways in which people with intellectual disabilities push us to be aware of profound questions about identity, community, and purpose. Vulnerability is all around us. Pretense and hidden feelings or thoughts are usually not characteristics of people marginalized because of disability or stigmatizing labels. The mythology is that we as caregivers or professionals are doing the helping and serving, when, in fact, those we serve and befriend are giving life to us as well (i.e., in addition to our jobs!). One of the strengths of the L'Arche communities and the work of Jean Vanier is that they name and claim, much more honestly and directly, the fact that the true human is found in community with those marginalized because of disability.

Parker Palmer talked about this shifting perspective from "giving" to "receiving" in a keynote address at a conference I organized in Rochester in 1986 on "Merging Two Worlds" (Palmer 1986). Palmer started the talk with reflections on understandings of community as a "gift we receive, not a goal we achieve," and the huge importance of "hospitality to the stranger" in the spiritual foundations of Christianity, Judaism, and Islam. The real gift is not from the host to the stranger but, potentially, from the stranger to the host, in that the stranger is often the messenger of God. Palmer summarized some other qualities of that call to hospitality by noting that there are at least three reasons why we are called to include and welcome the stranger. First, if the world is not safe for strangers, then it is not safe for me: I am a stranger to most others. Second, the stranger, as the one representing "diversity," saves us from the boredom of sameness. And third, we need multiple perspectives and points of view to see "truth." Accordingly, he notes a number of ways that people with developmental disabilities "puncture our illusions" about independence in a world full of dependence and interdependence, about our capacity to truly know someone else or ourselves, about our illusions of power and control over others, and about our capacity to escape our own diminishment and death.[2]

It is important to keep the relationship between "giving" and "receiving" in perspective, however, because there is a danger here. If living and working in community and serving with people with intellectual disabilities is indeed life-giving to those who feel called to those relationships, and if we are honest about what "they" have given us and how they have helped shape our vocation, the danger is that "their" value and worth, particularly people with severe disabilities, becomes that of helping us discover who we are. Is their vocation that of helping other people to understand what it means to be human, to come to terms with our projections, illusions, and self-deceptions, and to come into deeper and closer relationships with others and with God? If so, are they valued and compensated for that role? What if they want to contribute or serve in other ways that have nothing to do with my transformation? Is that why we celebrate them?

The reason I bring this up as a caveat is that I have had people with disabilities tell me that they would prefer that I not use them to work out my own issues. Of course, none of us can prevent other people from projecting or transferring their own personal, spiritual, or theological issues onto us. What's crucial is that we recognize what we are doing when that happens; that we be appropriately appreciative (by saying and acting so) for the teaching and guiding role that they have played with or without their knowing it; that we be very careful about the possibility of using people with disabilities for our own good; and that we then rededicate ourselves to relationships that enable them (and us) to work together on mutual understandings of vocation and call. That kind of mutual growth, in relationships of support, service, and friendship, is at the heart of the love, motivation, and sense of calling that we can see in the best of relationships between people with intellectual disabilities and those who live with, work with, and befriend them.

---

2. The power of Parker Palmer's presentation, and some of his subsequent work in the understanding of vocation and teaching, is that this talk came at a time when he had recently struggled through a period of major clinical depression. He clearly connected his story with his reflections about the "strangers" with labeled disabilities. The people who were willing to be with him in community, people who did not try to fix him, were part of his journey to recovery. For me, it was a transformative moment because the vocation of helping people with disabilities to find and claim their own identity within the wider community and the faith community was reframed in the much older call to be hospitable to the stranger rather than an overprofessionalized specialization of "serving the disabled."

From Celebrating Personhood to Identity in Community

Right behind Who am I? is the question Whose am I? As I try to answer the former question with words that define me or others, I will inevitably use adjectives indicating the qualities that I feel are unique to me, but that, in fact, connect me with others. For example, I like to garden. So do many others, and thus two potential sources of community for me are my local garden shop and the farmer's market. There are many other "connecting" characteristics about me that are communal: for example, American Baptist, Caucasian, professor, minister, and so on. I would submit that people with disabilities raise our awareness of the many ways of our connectedness to others because of the profound ways in which the quality of their lives depends on the care and support of others. We build systems of support and service to help so-called dependent people develop more independence; but in the process of getting to know them as individuals, we become more profoundly aware of how all of our lives are *interdependent.*

As professionals and friends of people with developmental disabilities in general have become more aware of the limiting power of labels, and of the gifts and strengths often hidden by those labels, the shift has been increasingly away from deficit-based assessment and planning to processes that see a disability as a function of the relationship between people and their environment, and, secondly, identify people by their strengths, gifts, and likes and dislikes as much as by their limitations. These person-centered planning processes essentially accept the disability as a given. It needs support and service, but it won't be fixed or cured. More often than not, it is not the disability that causes suffering but the attitudes by which it is approached, the lack of access and opportunity, and the lack of resources — all of which follow from a nonresponding environment. The disability itself is not all that defines the person. There are many other things that are important to the person — things she likes, things she wants to do. In the person-centered planning process she is telling us: "That's who I am. Help me grow into that."

Thus the focus becomes finding and building on strengths, preferences, and gifts. The implications of transferring that kind of assessment and planning to other areas of human need and service are just immense, for disability is just one small area where people with limitations are too often seen only in terms of their deficits, not their strengths, for example, as "the poor," "the elderly," "the uneducated," and so forth.

Most of the people with disabilities that I know also want to know that their lives make a difference, or they want a chance to pursue values and dreams and desires. At one of the Developmental Disabilities Lecture series that the Boggs Center coordinates in New Jersey, Lynne Seagle, executive director of Horizons (a creative community-based agency supporting people with intellectual disabilities in Virginia), noted that, when you boil down all the assessments and interviews and planning processes, adults with whom Horizons works want three things: a place they can call their own; something to do that is valued; and someone to love and who will love them (Seagle 2006). To express it another way, they want a sense of valued identity and a sense of belonging in relationships of love and care. This is very different from answering the question Whose are you? by stating that the person is a client of this or that agency and needs support for this or that disabling condition.

How?

Having shifted the question to the ways in which connectedness and community help to identify who people with disabilities are and what their lives are about, the task is then to raise the question of how we can achieve this. How can the relationships that connect them and include them in a community be recognized, affirmed, celebrated, and sustained? Again, people with developmental disabilities help us clarify the questions of what it means to serve and support others over time, when the issues or needs calling for that service or support cannot be fixed, cured, or eliminated. Here is where the disabled become the canaries in the mines of medical and human service.

What we are learning in this context is that good and effective support depends on a balancing and blending of both *formal* health and human services with what are called *informal*, or "natural," supports. An overreliance on formal caregiving systems leads to the isolation of institutions, an absence of friends, and the inordinate costs of trying to replicate experiences that make for quality of life in so-called typical communities. An overreliance on informal systems can also lead to isolation and overburdened families and caregiving systems, exhausting both the spiritual and financial resources for care and support. The two questions I see emerging here are: How do we most effectively share the caring between individual, family, friends, and public systems? And then the eternal question for families is: Who cares after I am gone?

This is where the L'Arche communities have so much to offer in terms of the power of their vision and the symbol of what so many families want for their sons or daughters when they are no longer able to care for them. Who's going to care for them in the same way we have? Who will know them, see them, be committed to them over the long haul, provide stability — and indeed love them? Who are their friends, those who will pledge to be there even if they are not paid? In the midst of large systems of residential services, supported living, and secular supports, the search I so often hear in families is for that sense of spiritual commitment to relationship and connection. That does not mean one can manufacture or mass-produce L'Arche communities. (That is something the L'Arche network knows only too well, and it is one of the reasons for their caution about growth that reaches beyond the capacity of the spirit and commitment to sustain relationships over the long haul and honor the promises made in the covenants with their core members.) But it could lead to collaborative partnerships between the public sphere, families, and faith communities, partnerships that pay attention to and honor spiritual dimensions of caregiving, build and protect long-term relationships, and sustain those doing the direct care in both body and soul by providing livable wages and other supports that reduce the dissonance between the vocation they have found and the value it is given in the public arena.

The creative answers to those questions that I see emerging are ones that listen carefully to individuals and families, to both the needs and dreams they have, so that public supports can be provided in ways that are tailor-made to individuals and their levels of need. They are ones where responsibility is shared, where individuals with disabilities are expected to use the gifts they have, where families and other informal support-givers are supported and sustained, and where professional services are provided in ways that keep the locus of control and choice, as much as possible, in the hands of the individuals and those who are closest to them in their care and support. In the United States, that kind of system blends the best of what is called "liberal" and "conservative" approaches. Those are systems that we in the United States call individualized funding or self-directed services, ones that also provide safety nets and places for people whose networks of relationships have been shattered for one reason or another. They are systems of care that pay intentional attention to "circles of support," a blending and broadening of the range of formal and informal relationships in someone's life. They are systems of care where the motivation and vocation at the heart of many who are called to work with people with disabilities is recognized, encouraged, and sustained, giving people the opportunity to reflect on and talk about why they do what they do. Finally, they are systems where the formal caregivers are forever cognizant of the difference between caregiving and friendships, and thus they recognize that part of their role is community building, that is, to facilitate, nurture, and sustain the kinds of relationships, connections, and experiences that build quality of life — in the best sense of that term.

Thus the issues in those circles of support and individualized plans become not just how people's limits because of their disability are met or treated, or how they have accomplished a new goal in behavior, daily living skills, or employment, but also who and where their friends are. How do we help them keep in contact and connection and participation with others who have come to know, accept, and love them just as they are — not for what they might become — where they know they have the opportunity to serve, to help, and know that they make a difference in the lives of others? That may be as simple as a recent innovation by a chaplain at a New Jersey facility who is presenting certificates of appreciation for the gifts that staff see in the lives of individuals with severe disabilities at their annual planning meeting, a symbolic act that reframes the system of serving them into one of mutuality and valued interdependence.

The answers to the "how" of celebration and belonging presume answers to the question of where care is best provided, where people belong, and when it should happen. For relationships and opportunities for participation and connection to happen, people with developmental disabilities belong as close to the community as possible, in systems of support that can sustain individual relationships and connection and spark new ones by more opportunities for connection and relationship. They belong in our neighborhoods, at our congregational worship services, and in community celebrations. Unless they have the opportunity to participate, people with disabilities will remain a class of people rather than becoming James, John, Susan, and Diane, individuals with unique interests, gifts, and needs, individuals whom others find themselves drawn to because of something that is being stirred within them. One of the fellow congregants of Lior Liebling, a young man with Down syndrome known for his capacity to lead his synagogue in prayer in Philadelphia, noted that Lior "answered questions for me I never knew I had."[3]

In summary, the questions about what it means to be and celebrate

---

3. www.prayingwithlior.com. See also Le Pichon, preceding chapter.

what is human, and what it means to be community, get clarified. Theologically, we in the Judaeo-Christian tradition declare and affirm that this value comes from creation in the image of God and belonging to the body of Christ, or the people of God. Who are you? A child of God. Whose are you? One of "God's people." What am I to do? To serve and follow, to make a difference, in the best way I can. And that goes for people with developmental disabilities just as much as for the people who are called to serve them.

References

Moltmann, J. 1983. The liberation and acceptance of the handicapped. In *The power of the powerless,* 137-54. San Francisco: Harper and Row.

Palmer, P. 1986. Merging two worlds. Keynote address at conference in Rochester, New York. AAIDD Religion and Spirituality Division. DVD. New Brunswick, NJ: The Elizabeth M. Boggs Center on Developmental Disabilities (www.rwjms.umdnj.edu/boggscenter).

Seagle, L. 2006. Self-directed supports: A provider's perspective. Lecture in the Developmental Disabilities Lectures Series, New Brunswick, NJ: The Elizabeth M. Boggs Center on Developmental Disabilities (www.rwjms.umdnj.edu/boggscenter).

Chapter Nine

Seeing Peace: L'Arche as a Peace Movement

Stanley Hauerwas

How L'Arche Makes Peace Visible

One of the gifts L'Arche offers Christians and non-Christians alike is that it enables us to visualize peace. Some may find this remark odd since L'Arche did not begin as a peace movement; furthermore, the primary work of L'Arche does not seem to be about peace. Moreover, apart from questions about L'Arche, there is the matter of *seeing* peace. Why do we need to *see* peace? We need to see peace because we have been taught that violence is the norm and peace the exception. In calling attention to L'Arche as a peace movement, therefore, I hope to show that peace is not an ideal waiting to be realized. Rather, peace is as real — as concrete — as the work of L'Arche. By seeing the realization of peace in the communities of L'Arche, we are better able to see and enact peace in our own lives.

Christianity, like peace, is not an idea; rather, it is a bodily faith that must be seen to be believed. As we pray following the Eucharist, we "eat this body" and "drink this blood" so that we might become "living members of your Son our savior, Jesus Christ." We partake of the bread and wine as the body and blood of Christ because in doing so we are taken up into Christ's vision of his creation. Given this vision, we look for Christ's presence in the world to help us live into our calling as members of his body. L'Arche, a community built on faith, turns out to be a lens that helps us see God's peace in the world.

In suggesting that L'Arche is a peace movement, I do not think I am forcing a category on L'Arche, or on Jean Vanier. Vanier has increasingly identified working for peace to be one of the primary purposes of L'Arche. The same is true for the various zones of L'Arche around the world. For example, the recent newsletter of L'Arche USA Zone identified its "zone mandate" by focusing on four major themes:

Fostering vocation in L'Arche by continuing to build structures and processes that support long-term membership in our communities

Announcing L'Arche and the gifts of people with disabilities in order to help build a more peaceful and just world

Deepening our relationships of solidarity within the Federation of L'Arche, especially with our communities in Latin America and the Caribbean

Exploring new models for living the Mission that respond to current realities facing our communities (L'Arche USA 2006, 2)

It is by no means clear, however, how "announcing" the gifts of people with disabilities can help "build a more peaceful and just world." The phrase "in order" in the second theme seems to suggest a causal connection between the work of L'Arche and the work of peace, but it remains vague as to how we should understand the relationship between those two tasks. Nor is it apparent how the four themes are interrelated. How does building structures and processes that support long-term vocations serve to sustain a more peaceful world? Why is "deepening our relationships of solidarity within the Federation of L'Arche" so important, particularly as the work of peace?

I believe that there are good answers to these questions to be found in the work of Jean Vanier. Accordingly, by drawing on his work, I will try to spell out how Vanier understands L'Arche to be a movement for peace. I should warn the reader that, as I do so, Vanier's ideas will often sound very much like John Howard Yoder's understanding of Christian nonviolence. I do not think that is accidental, because Jean Vanier and John Howard Yoder do strike many of the same chords, though in quite different keys.[1]

Vanier, particularly after September 11, 2001, has increasingly and explicitly emphasized that one of the essential tasks of L'Arche is to exemplify peace. With his usual insight into the complex character of our lives, he of-

---

1. Yoder is perhaps best known for his book *The Politics of Jesus: Vicit Agnus Noster* (Grand Rapids: Eerdmans, 1995). It would be extremely interesting to do a close comparison of Yoder's and Vanier's reading of Scripture.

ten calls attention to fear as the source of our violence. The fear that dominates our lives is not in the first instance the fear of an enemy, unless it is acknowledged that each of us is the enemy; rather, the fear that is the source of violence is the same fear that makes us unwilling to acknowledge the wounded character of our lives.[2] L'Arche, a place where the wounds of each person cannot avoid being exposed and thus, we hope, healed, becomes a context where we can learn the patient habits necessary for being at peace. Vanier knows that such an understanding of peace may not have results for creating a more peaceful world at the international level, but he suggests that "we are all called to become men and women of peace wherever we may be — in our family, at work, in our parish, in our neighborhood" (quoted in Spink 2006, 225).

Though Vanier's modesty about the work of L'Arche not being a strategy designed to end the scourge of war is admirable, I want to suggest that L'Arche is exactly the kind of peace work we so desperately need if our imaginations are to be capable of conceiving what peace might look like at the international level.[3] One of the problems with being an advocate of peace — and I am a pacifist — is the widespread presumption that violence is the rule and peace the exception. The pacifist, therefore, is assumed to bear the burden of proof, because violence is thought to be necessary for the maintenance of a relatively just and secure order. The question addressed to the pacifist, "What would you do if . . . ?" allegedly shows the unworkability of a commitment to peace. L'Arche is the way I believe that question must be answered.[4]

---

2. Scott Bader-Saye (2007) explains how fear possesses the lives of Americans, making us incapable of following Jesus. Bell (2007) offers an equally compelling case that helps us see how liberal politics is not about the dissipation of a prepolitical fear, but about the production and manipulation of fear.

3. Vanier (2005, 43) makes the strong claim that those who become a friend of the weak will be blessed by God by discovering that the gospel is truly "good news," that is, "it is a solution to the deep wounds of humanity, a way to stop the cycle of violence and war." So he does think the work of L'Arche has implications for what an alternative to war might look like. For example, I cannot help but think that if the president of the United States spent one day a week in a L'Arche home, he could not help but think twice about his assumption that war is inevitable.

4. For a more direct response to the challenge, see Yoder (1983). Yoder challenges the deterministic presumptions often behind the question "What would you do if . . . ?" observing that if I have told myself beforehand that there are no alternatives other than violence, then I am not forced to find imaginative and creative alternatives. L'Arche, I believe, is the exemplification of Yoder's point. Who could have imagined L'Arche if Vanier had assumed

Vanier and the work of L'Arche help us see that peace is a deeper reality than violence. However, this vision — a vision that enables us to see that peace is a deeper reality than violence because we were created to be at peace — requires training. It turns out that our teachers are the core members of L'Arche, and their gift is their unprotected vulnerability.[5] In learning to live with those whom we call "the disabled," we learn to recognize that questions such as "Would it not have been better if a person so disabled would not have been born?" are not questions we are tempted to ask if we have learned to view our world through the lens L'Arche provides. For the answers, even the most humane answers, to such questions too often disguise a violence cloaked in the language of compassion.[6]

The Mystery of Suffering

I need to explain this last remark, because it is important for understanding the kind of peace found in L'Arche. Crucial for our learning to be at peace with ourselves and one another is the ability to accept the mystery of suffering. But it turns out that that is exactly what we have lost the ability to do.

In an extraordinary but unfortunately not well-known book, *Victims and Values: A History and a Theory of Suffering,* J. A. Amato argues that modernity is marked fundamentally by a transformation of how suffering is understood and responded to (Amato 1990). Amato observes that all hu-

---

there was no alternative to institutionalizing those with developmental disabilities. Yoder asks, "Does not the Christian belief in resurrection — not simply as one bygone event but as God's pattern of action in human experience — mean that it is precisely where we do not see how a situation can possibly be worked out that God might demonstrate his saving intent?" (1983, 34).

5. See Müller-Fahrenholz (2007) for an extraordinary analysis of how an acknowledgment of vulnerability could lead to a more imaginative and "effective" foreign policy.

6. Bader-Saye (2006, 103-4) observes that if we attend to Scripture, we must observe that ordinarily God does not choose to prevent evil and suffering, but to redeem it. Accordingly, the real question is not determining "why" something happened but what kind of response is appropriate if we are to participate in God's redemptive work. Bader-Saye suggests that "providence is a way of giving time a story that invites a certain kind of politics. Trust in divine provision makes possible risky ventures of vulnerable love because we trust that the end of the story is in God's hands and not ours. We have been freed from the pressure of making history turn out right and thus have been set free to live the generosity, peacefulness, and hospitality that correspond to God's gracious and plentiful provision."

man cultures must give meaning to suffering, but a fundamental shift in attitudes toward suffering occurred in the Enlightenment. The shift was characterized by a social sympathy for those who suffer, which led to reform movements that resulted in much social good. But that same sympathy, when confronted by more victims than can be cared for, also led to a battle over the value of suffering.

Just at the time when people developed a universal sympathy for all those who suffer — thus the significance given to the status of being a victim — they also increasingly came to believe that suffering is not an inevitable part of human experience. And thus the presumption shared by increasing numbers of people that it is wrong not to be happy. Jeremy Bentham exemplifies this attitude in his attempt to develop a social calculus that aims to do nothing less than remove all unnecessary suffering from human experience (Amato 1990, 79). However, hidden in this humanism is a violence against all who suffer in such a way that their suffering cannot be eliminated.[7] Hence, in the name of sympathy for the sufferer, we must eliminate those who cannot be "cured." It is against this violence that Vanier sets his face by insisting on the mystery of suffering. He observes:

> Jesus did not come into the world to explain suffering nor to justify its existence. He came to reveal that we can all alleviate pain, through our competence and our compassion. He came to show us that every pain, every hurt we experience can become an offering, and thus a source of life for others in and through Jesus' offering of love to the Father. (Vanier 2005, 89)[8]

---

7. We are all, of course, subject to suffering that cannot be eliminated because we are all destined to die — thus the death-denying character of so much of our lives as "modern people." Amato (1990, 20) observes that "death ruptures our ethical world. It creates a discrepancy between what is intended and what is achieved, between what is offered and what is accepted. Death makes injustice permanent."

8. I had first thought to use this occasion to explore some of the connections between Wittgenstein's and Vanier's work. I discovered, however, as I tried to write about those connections, that the story was far too complicated for a short essay. However, I think Wittgenstein's remarks concerning language games is very important if we are to understand the work of L'Arche and Vanier's understanding of that work. For example, Wittgenstein says: "The origin and the primitive form of the language game is a reaction; only from this can more complicated forms develop. Language — I want to say — is a refinement, in the beginning was the deed" (1980, 31e). Accordingly, Wittgenstein reminds us that when justifications reach bedrock, "my spade is turned. Then I am inclined to say: 'This

Vanier's great gift, the gift of L'Arche, is to teach us to see pain, to enter into the pain of others, without wanting to destroy those who suffer.[9] In *Befriending the Stranger,* Vanier tells the story of Lucien, who was born with severe mental and physical disabilities. He could not talk, and his twisted body meant that he had to spend his life in a wheelchair or the bed. He lived the first thirty years of his life with his mother, who could interpret his body language.[10] He was at peace with his mother, but he fell ill and required hospitalization. When he lost all points of reference, screams of anguish possessed him. He came to "La Forestiere," but his constant screaming continued and nothing seemed to work to calm him. Vanier confesses that Lucien's screams pierced the very core of his being, forcing him to recognize that he would be willing to hurt Lucien to keep him quiet. Vanier

---

is simply what I do'" (1953, 217). The work of L'Arche is bedrock, and Vanier tries to help us see that "this is simply what he does." It is as if Vanier, who I suspect has never read Wittgenstein, understood intuitively Wittgenstein's admonition that "we must do away with all *explanation,* and description alone must take its place" (1953, 109). Vanier never tries to explain — at least he never tries to understand — a particular action and practice as the exemplification or application of a universal idea, but rather he does the only thing he can do, that is, he holds before us the lives that have shaped his life, which means that he helps us see bedrock by telling stories of L'Arche. Stories are all we have if it is true that Jesus did not come to explain suffering. Amato observes: "Nothing so denies us and our stories, as the denial of our sufferings and sacrifices. If we have no sufferings or sacrifices to call our own, we have no story to tell, and with no story to tell, we are no people at all" (1990, 210)

9. Amato provides a close analysis of the difference, as well as the interrelated character, of pain and suffering. He observes: "Suffering is greater and more comprehensive than pain. Suffering describes a general condition, person, group, or society. While not impossible, it would be unusual to speak of the many sufferings of a person's pain, whereas we commonly speak of suffering as if it is composed of many pains. Suffering does not invite specific and immediate remedies" (Amato 1990, 15).

10. The significance of the body as language, and particularly the language of pain, for Vanier again suggests some fascinating connections with Wittgenstein. For example, Wittgenstein remarks: "I want to regard man here as an animal; as a primitive being to which one grants instinct but not ratiocination. As a creature in a primitive state. Any logic good enough for a primitive means of communication needs no apology from us. Language did not emerge from some kind of ratiocination" (1969, 475). By "primitive," Wittgenstein does not mean a contrast with "civilized," but rather to remind us, as he says later, "You must bear in mind that the language-game (how water behaves when boiled or frozen) is to say something unpredictable. I mean: it is not based on grounds. It is not reasonable (or unreasonable). It is there — like life" (1969, 559). L'Arche is the extended training necessary to learning the language of the body and pain. The people who speak that language, a language whose "words" are often gestures of the body, do not need to be explained. They are there — like life. Our task is to learn to listen to what they have to say.

had to recognize that he, someone who thought he had been called to share his life with the weak, had in his heart the capacity to hate a weak person (Vanier 2005, 62; see also chap. 1 above).

The work of L'Arche is dangerous as it tempts us to rage against those we are committed to "help." So when Vanier tells us that "it is important to enter into the mystery of pain, the pain of our brothers and sisters in countries that are at war, the pain of our brothers and sisters who are sick, who are hungry, and who are in prison," he puts us at great risk (Vanier 2005, 87). To face the mystery of pain means that we must confront the violence we harbor in our hearts, violence created by a world we cannot force to conform to our desires. Vanier suggests: "The only thing that matters is that we be truthful; that we do not let ourselves be governed by lies and by illusion" (Vanier 2005, 61).[11] But to face the truth about ourselves — the truth that we desire to eliminate those in pain — is no easy task. Yet without such truth there can be no peace.

The Politics of Peace

In order to understand how L'Arche could be a peace movement, one must recognize L'Arche as a politics. L'Arche may not seem to represent the kind of political engagement often associated with movements for a more peaceable world, but any movement for peace not determined by L'Arche-like politics will only threaten to become a form of violence. Let me try to explain this enigmatic remark. Some years ago, when many were concerned that the Cold War might result in a nuclear holocaust, I wrote an article against the presumption that "peace" could be equated with human survival and against the correlative implication being drawn by some that all life should be organized to ensure that nuclear weapons were elimi-

---

11. Vanier (2004, 160) observes that "the truth is often hidden from us, which is why it takes time and the help of others to discern the truth. We often find truth only after we choose to let go of some of the illusions of life we may still have. It takes time to find inner freedom — this is the ongoing work of a lifetime. I do not have this freedom yet, but my hope is to continue to keep my heart open to receive it. Even though truth makes us free, we never *possess* it. We are called humbly to contemplate the truth that is given us, to search unceasingly in order to be drawn into truth, to let ourselves be led, in the company of others, into the unfolding mystery of truth, to be possessed by truth and to serve truth. To live in truth is to live a relationship of love with the Word of God made flesh, who is truth, compassion and forgiveness."

nated. The title of the article was "Taking Time for Peace: The Moral Significance of the Trivial." There I argued:

> Peace takes time. Put even more strongly, peace creates time by its steadfast refusal to force the other to submit in the name of order. Peace is not a static state but an activity which requires constant attention and care. An activity by its very nature takes place over time. In fact, activity creates time, as we know how to characterize duration only by noting that we did this first, and then this second, and so on, until we either get somewhere or accomplish this or that task. So peace is the process through which we make time our own rather than be determined by "events" over which, it is alleged, we have no control. (Hauerwas 1988, 258)[12]

I do not think that, at the time I wrote "Taking Time for Peace," I was familiar with the work of Jean Vanier or L'Arche. But once I discovered Vanier and L'Arche, I thought I saw what peace must surely look like. If I was right that the politics of peace is a politics of time, then L'Arche is truly a fine exemplification of that. For at the heart of L'Arche is patience, which turns out to be but another name for peace (Yoder 1999). To join L'Arche at any level requires that you be ready to be slowed down. It is not just "all right" to take two hours to eat a meal with a core member, or even longer to bathe a body not easily "handled," but L'Arche requires that those who do this important work learn that time is not a zero-sum game. We have all the time we need to do what needs to be done (Hauerwas 1999).

L'Arche also teaches the significance of place. Assistants should not be constantly going and coming. Core members love routines, and routines create and are created by familiarity, and familiarity makes place "a" place. Place and routine can become boring without the celebration of beauty. Thus it is crucial for L'Arche that each person's birthday be celebrated in recognition of the beauty that is their life. Place and routine are transformed by recognizing the beauty of each person. And this celebration of

---

12. In the letter that invited us to Trosly, we were asked to address the "ontological issues related to the difference between 'being' and 'doing.'" There are metaphysical presumptions involved in this paragraph, but they challenge the presumption that ontologically being and doing are two "things." If Aquinas is right, and I certainly think he is, being is activity (Burrell 1979, 45-48). It is crucial to avoid "intellectualistic" accounts of activity, that is, the view that for an action to be an action it must be caused by "reason." The body has its reasons, making action possible.

each life makes trust possible, thereby making L'Arche possible. So Zone USA was right: there is a connection between building structures and processes that support long-term membership in L'Arche communities and the process through which a more peaceful and just world can come into being. Without L'Arche and communities like L'Arche, we could not know what trust in its most determinative form looks like.

Alasdair MacIntyre suggests that, if I am to be a trustworthy person, I must be able to be relied on even when it may be to my advantage to betray another's trust or when it may be inconvenient for me to be relied on. Therefore, trust requires that we are able to trust one another not only in the routines of everyday life, but particularly when we are a burden by reason of our disabilities. Those who have learned to trust us must know that we will be there in times and places we have promised to be, even when to be so is costly (MacIntyre 1999, 109-10).[13] Interestingly enough, Vanier has taught us that we learn to trust from those whom we first thought must come to trust us. Mutual vulnerability makes a trust between assistant and core member possible that is otherwise unimaginable.

Moreover, such trust not only makes possible but necessary, as L'Arche Zone USA suggests, the task to deepen its relationship with other L'Arche communities in other parts of the world. I often call attention to a Mennonite poster that has this slogan: "A Modest Proposal for Peace — Let the Christians of the World Agree They Will Not Kill One Another." Peace is to know others in a way that makes impossible any thought of their destruction in the interest of "wider loyalties." It is hard to imagine anyone who has lived in a L'Arche community thinking that violence must be used in the name of a "good cause." The timefulness and placedness of a L'Arche way of life provides an alternative to the violence of the world shaped by speed and placelessness. And it is just such a world in which we find ourselves. For if Paul Virilio is right, the dominant form violence takes in modernity is speed. According to Virilio, contemporary war is shaped by mechanisms of mass communication that make war less and less about territory and more and more about the management of information (Virilio 1990). As a result, our perceptions are mediated by the logic of violence in the form of speed creating a new

13. MacIntyre has learned much from Logstrup's account of trust as a central feature arising spontaneously from our relationships with one another. Yet he thinks Logstrup fails to distinguish between the initial trust of children, some element which is preserved throughout our lives, and mature trust for which we can sometimes give good reasons (MacIntyre 2007).

vision of the world in which all people "naturally" understand themselves to be part of the war machine. Local space and time disappear, to be replaced by a single, global, and virtual "real time." This, according to Virilio, is "what the doctrine of security is founded on: the saturation of time and space by speed, making daily life the last theater of operations, the ultimate scene of strategic foresight" (Virilio 1990, 92; see also Huebner 2006, 119-20).

Huebner argues that Virilio's account of violence as speed helps us see why peace cannot simply be understood as an alternative to war. Too often such alternatives reproduce the violence hidden in the very terms we use to underwrite a peace that is no more than the absence of overt hostilities. Rather, what is needed is a community, a people, who are shaped by practices that force them to acknowledge that God has given them all the time in the world — a world that thinks it has no time to receive peace as a gift. Huebner argues, I think quite rightly, that John Howard Yoder's non-Constantinian understanding of the church helps us see what such a people might look like (Huebner 2006, 126-32).[14] I am suggesting that, in a similar way, L'Arche is a community that is necessary to train us to see the difficult but happy work that peace is.

Vanier is surely right that the only thing that matters is that we be truthful. A "peace" that is anything less than truthful cannot but hide from us the violence we perpetrate in the name of peace. Commenting on Yoder's epistemology of nonviolence, Huebner observes that truthfulness is an utterly contingent gift that can only be given because truth "emerges at the site of vulnerable interchange with the other" (Huebner 2006, 126). "Vulnerable interchange with the other" is certainly as good a description of L'Arche as we can have.

The Witness of L'Arche In and To the World

Yet Vanier believes that the peace we see in L'Arche cannot be limited to L'Arche, because we are creatures created to be at peace with ourselves and one another. According to Vanier:

14. I find it quite interesting that Vanier has increasingly become critical of Constantinian developments in which "Church and State became intertwined," and as a result building huge and beautiful buildings became more important than "being attentive to the poor and seeing them at the heart of the church" (Vanier 2004, 236).

Absolutely everything is engraved in our being. So the experience of being loved by God does not change our lives completely, yet something is changed when we realize that God loves us just as we are, not as we would like to be nor as our parents or society would have liked us to be. (Vanier 2005, 32)[15]

Vanier's confidence that L'Arche but manifests the peace that is engraved in our being is correlative of his conviction that God, through the mystery of the incarnation, has entered into our very being (Vanier 2005, 55). That is why suffering does not need to be explained, for what has been given to us is not an explanation but the practice of charity through which we are drawn into the very life of God. That practice, the practice of charity, Vanier often identifies with learning not just to wash the feet of people with disabilities but to have our feet washed by them. By having our feet washed by them, we may begin to recognize that we must first learn to receive if we are to give. A receiving, moreover, that requires that we acknowledge our own wounds.[16]

The christological center that shapes Vanier's understanding of the work of L'Arche is why he burns with a passion to be in conversation with those from other faiths or no faith. For him, such a conversation is possible because of what he has learned by having his feet washed by the disabled. In a letter to L'Arche he reports on the meeting organized by the community of Sant'Egidio to celebrate the first international meeting called in 1996 by Pope John Paul II. Muslim leaders, Jewish rabbis, and Christian bishops came together "to share and pray for peace and to be a sign of

15. It would be fascinating to explore Vanier's understanding of these matters with regard to the debates occasioned by de Lubac's understanding of the relationship of nature and grace. My hunch is that Vanier might exemplify de Lubac's insistence that grace is not extrinsically related to nature but rather is a gift that makes possible a narrative of our lives otherwise unavailable. This is an extremely important matter because I fear that some may confuse Vanier's Christian humanism with a secular humanism that is the antithesis of the gospel. John Milbank provides a good account of de Lubac's Christian humanism (Milbank 2005, 9-11).

16. Vanier reports a lesson he learned from a letter he read written by the psychologist Carl Jung (Vanier has a genius for learning from people I distrust and dislike). Jung observed that he admired Christians for seeing Jesus in the hungry and thirsty, but what he did not understand was Christians' failure to see Jesus in their own poverty. Christians, it seems, always want to do good to the poor who are outside ourselves, but we often deny the poor person that resides in our own lives. This led Vanier to acknowledge that he could not help Lucien unless and until he was open to and ready to accept his own wounds and seek help — a help that comes from the very ones that Vanier sought to help (Vanier 2005, 64).

peace and of prayer." Vanier participated in a workshop on "the love of God and the love of people," in which he shared the life of "Ghadir, a young Muslim girl with severe disabilities whom we had welcomed in our L'Arche community near Bethany and how my encounter with her had been a sign of God and a place of transformation for me." That Ghadir exists means it just may be possible for Muslims and Christians to discover common work necessary for us to be at peace.

In an earlier essay on the work of Vanier and L'Arche, entitled "The Politics of Gentleness," I have suggested that L'Arche cannot be L'Arche if it loses its animating center, that is, faith in Jesus as the one who has redeemed time (Hauerwas and Coles 2008). Of course, there is the possibility of L'Arche communities that are shaped by other religious or nonreligious convictions. But they are possible because a Jean Vanier exists to exemplify what happens to a life that has learned what it means to have one's feet washed by the least of these.[17] In this respect, the work of L'Arche is analogous to John Howard Yoder's understanding of "the pacifism of the Messianic community," which affirms

> . . . its dependence upon the confession that Jesus is Christ and that Jesus Christ is Lord. To say that Jesus is the Messiah is to say that in him are fulfilled the expectations of God's people regarding the one in whom God's will would perfectly be done. Therefore, in the person and work of Jesus, in his teachings and his passion, this kind of pacifism finds its rootage, and in his resurrection it finds its enablement. (Yoder 1992, 133-34)

Yoder notes that one of the disadvantages of such a pacifism is that it cannot promise to "work" (Yoder 1992, 137). Yet I take it that that is exactly what this understanding of peace shares with the work of L'Arche. For L'Arche does not claim to "work," but rather to be the exemplification of what would be missed if we only tried what is assumed to work. Such a witness, however, can only be sustained if a people exist who are shaped by the understanding that their work only makes sense because they have seen peace in the body and blood of Christ. So also our vision must be trained to recognize Christ's peace when we see it in the work of people like Jean Vanier and communities like L'Arche. That is why I think it so important that we see the peace that is L'Arche.

17. This way of putting the matter I owe to Dan Morehead.

References

Amato, J. A. 1990. *Victims and values: A history and a theory of suffering.* New York: Praeger.

Bader-Saye, S. 2007. *Following Jesus in a culture of fear.* Grand Rapids: Brazos Press.

———. 2006. Figuring time: Providence and politics. In *Liturgy, time, and the politics of redemption,* ed. R. Rashkover and C. C. Pecknold, 91-111. Grand Rapids: Eerdmans.

Bell, D. 2007. The politics of fear and the gospel of life. *Journal for Cultural and Religious Theory* 8 (2): 55-80.

Burrell, D. 1979. *Aquinas: God and action.* London: Routledge and Kegan Paul.

Hauerwas, S. M. 1988. Taking time for peace: The moral significance of the trivial. In *Christian existence today: Essays on church, world, and living in between,* 253-66. Durham: Labyrinth Press; reprint (2001) Grand Rapids: Brazos Press.

———. 1999. Timeful friends: Living with the handicapped. In *Sanctify them in the truth: Holiness exemplified,* 143-56. Nashville: Abingdon Press.

Hauerwas, S. M., and R. Coles. 2008. *Christianity, democracy, and the radical ordinary: Conversations between a radical Democrat and a Christian.* Eugene, OR: Cascade Books.

Huebner, C. 2006. *A precarious peace: Yoderian explorations on theology, knowledge, and identity.* Scottdale, PA: Herald Press.

L'Arche USA. 2006. *The journey and the dream* 8, no. l (December).

MacIntyre, A. 1999. *Dependent rational animals.* Chicago: Open Court.

———. 2007. Human nature and human dependence: What might a Thomist learn from reading Logstrup? In *Concern for the other: Perspectives on the ethics of K. E. Logstrup,* ed. Sven Andersen and Kees van Kooten Niekerk, 147-66. Notre Dame, IN: University of Notre Dame Press.

Milbank, J. 2005. *The suspended middle: Henri de Lubac and the debate concerning the supernatural.* Grand Rapids: Eerdmans.

Müller-Fahrenholz, G. 2007. What if? The missed opportunity of 9/11. *Christian Century* 124 (1): 30-34.

Spink, K. 2006. *The miracle, the message, the story: Jean Vanier and L'Arche.* Mahwah, NJ: HiddenSpring.

Vanier, J. 2005. *Befriending the stranger.* Grand Rapids: Eerdmans.

———. 2004. *Drawn into the mystery of Jesus through the Gospel of John.* New York: Paulist Press.

Virilio, P. 1990. *Popular defense and ecological struggles.* New York: Semiotext(e).

Wittgenstein, L. 1953. *Philosophical investigations.* New York: Macmillan.

———. 1969. *On certainty.* New York: Harper Torchbooks.

———. 1980. *Culture and value.* Chicago: University of Chicago Press.

Yoder, J. H. 1983. *What would you do?* Scottdale, PA: Herald Press.

————. 1992. *Nevertheless: Varieties of religious pacifism.* Scottdale, PA: Herald Press.

————. 1995. *The politics of Jesus: Vicit agnus noster.* Grand Rapids: Eerdmans.

————. 1999. "Patience" as a method in moral reasoning: Is an ethic of discipleship "absolute"? In *The wisdom of the cross: Essays in honor of John Howard Yoder,* ed. S. Hauerwas, C. Huebner, H. Huebner, and M. Thiessen Nation, 24-42. Grand Rapids: Eerdmans.

Chapter Ten

Supererogation and the Riskiness of Human Vulnerability

Brian Brock

Introduction

What does it mean to *investigate* human fragility? And what counts as *knowledge* or *results* from such investigations? Theology and the empirical sciences will give different but related answers to these questions, answers that will, we hope, mutually illuminate one another (Brock, Dörfler, and Ulrich 2007).

Theologians and scientists pursue at least two strategies for answering these questions in this book. One investigative strategy is to rearrange cultural conditions so that people are made to feel vulnerable under controlled and observable conditions. Another is to seek out those places in our own cultures where people say they feel vulnerable as a mode of social analysis. Both are empirical investigations, differing only in whether they investigate by *creating* or simply by *discovering* people's existing sensations of vulnerability. As Hans Reinders has already reminded us in his introduction to this volume, the sensation of vulnerability is related in complex ways to the actual vulnerabilities produced by mental and physical impairments. If our interest is in analyzing our own societies, we must keep both aspects of this complex field of relationships in view. Hauerwas asks us to begin our exploration of human fragility by thinking theologically about one existing group of communities in which the interplay of these two forms of vulnerability is exposed, the L'Arche communities (preceding chap.). In so doing, Hauerwas seeks to learn what this way of life teaches us about how to live with fragility in all spheres of human existence. He studies L'Arche as a "given" to be understood, moving from there to suggest what kind of people we have to be if we are to take seriously the witness of that community of care. To attend to such a community of care, therefore, represents a discrete mode of investigating the virtues necessary to accept and live in solidarity with all human fragility.

In this chapter I investigate a conceptual complex from the discourse of medical ethics, which seems to set up barriers to the embrace of the vulnerable lives around which a community like L'Arche orbits. I will assess the role of the concept of "supererogation" from a theological perspective. Put in the simplest possible terms, my claim will be that, when used in the context of medical ethics, supererogation suggests that loving our family members with a disability, particularly when this involves our children, is somehow special — or more sacrificial — than loving other, "normal" people. My analysis will examine one very influential account of medical ethics, namely, the one presented by Tom Beauchamp and James Childress in *Principles of Biomedical Ethics*. I will suggest that the use of supererogation in their account fuels trajectories within Western medicine that seek to eliminate human vulnerability, and with it those human beings who are characterized as "defective." I hope to show that this use of "supererogation," in combination with conceptions of genetic risk, renders the carrying of a disabled fetus to term a heroic act, at best, and a callous one, at worst. I am not suggesting, of course, that the concept of supererogation as used in this textbook of medical ethics is *causally* operative in the process of eliminating vulnerability. Instead, I will draw out why this account of medical ethics has no internal resources to stand against a rising tide of resistance to human vulnerability in one particular field: prenatal testing. Before turning to supererogation, however, I will consider the practical context in which mothers and parents face questions of genetic risk and of the space of genetic counseling.

Being for and Bearing the Vulnerable: The Problem of Prenatal Testing

It is by now well documented that many pregnant women in highly medicalized Western societies feel strong, sometimes coercive resistance to their decisions not to abort what has been diagnosed as an "affected" fetus. Here the proximity of actual and felt vulnerability is particularly apparent. Leisa Whitaker, who has a form of dwarfism, relates her experience of prenatal genetic testing in terms only slightly more stark than that of many women.

> I remember sitting in the [genetic specialist's] rooms listening as he explained that there was a 25 percent chance that our child could still inherit the dominant achondroplasia gene and the dominant pseudo-achondroplasia gene — a combination that they had never seen before anywhere in the world. They had no idea of what effect this would have on the baby. . . . Having told us this the specialist offered us an abortion. He asked us to think about whether we wanted to bring another dwarf baby into the world. It was something I hadn't even thought of. This was our child! Why would we not want her? Why would the world not accept our child? (Tankard Reist 2006, 214)[1]

Rayna Rapp (2000) attempts to give some sociological purchase on the forces producing the medical "common sense" that would lead to the assumption that the reasonable course of action for a pregnant woman would be to abort a "defective" fetus. It draws on extensive anthropological research collected in the late 1980s and early 1990s on the main participants in the drama of amniocentesis in the city of New York. I will focus here on her findings regarding one of the many actors involved, the genetic counselor. Rapp found that genetic counselors play a prominent role in exposing the *conceptual* assumptions underpinning the view that bearing a disabled child is an irrational choice. What is simply assumed in related peri- and neonatal fields comes explicitly to expression in the work of the genetic counselor.

Genetic counseling is a subfield that grew from research genetics in the 1970s, and it took over the pastoral and educational task of linking the world of the scientific laboratory and that of parents. As Rapp suggests, their task is conceived of as primarily focused on counseling (Rapp 2000, 56-57), and it is directed toward the facilitation of nondirective value-neutral advice, with the stated purpose of assisting women's reproductive choice. Thus the basic aim of the discipline is on the surface straightforward: the genetic counselor provides information about hereditary risk to prospective parents. The practical task of the counselor is to prepare parents to take the test, and to explain the meaning of laboratory results. The

---

1. This volume collects nineteen first-person narratives by women who experienced medicalized pre- and postnatal care as antagonistic to the continuation of their pregnancies.

counseling session reflects four main goals in how it proceeds: to establish the primacy of scientific discourse, to establish the authority of this discourse, to communicate risk, and to construct a family history narrated in medicalized terms.

Establishing the primacy of scientific discourse involves explaining what chromosomes are, how they work, and how "defects" produce disabilities. In this sense, genetic counselors are science educators who simultaneously establish and maintain the authority of the scientific expert. Since the accuracy of the geneticist's diagnosis is the premise of the counselor's work, there is a strongly pro-expertise bias built into genetic counseling.

Explaining the functioning of chromosomes is a prelude to introducing the crucial concept of *risk*. This is thoroughly statistical territory, in which it is assumed that rationality and choice can be meaningfully tied to percentages of risk. The aim of the discourse of risk is to construct an "appropriate" or "numerically rational" sense of anxiety, which is tied to those features of procreation that are susceptible to genetic analysis. Genetic counseling is, Rapp continues, thoroughly wedded to this medicalized and statistical understanding of pregnancy.

> The technology of prenatal diagnosis was developed explicitly to allow the selection and abortion of fetuses facing serious disabilities because of atypical chromosomes and genes. The language of genetic counseling is intended to enhance awareness of the age-related risk of chromosomal problems, but counselors rarely speak directly about disability or abortion decisions unless a problem is detected. Counselors describe their goals quite differently: to give reassurance. . . . This language of "added risk," "background risk," and "reassurance" is consistently deployed by all the genetic counselors I have observed at work. It thus foregrounds a statistical, medical, age-related, universal and wholly individual model of risk. (Rapp 2000, 70)

Risk is communicated in more or less sophisticated ways, depending on the mother being addressed.

> To someone perceived as scientifically sophisticated, at Middle or Elite Hospitals: "At 35, a woman's risk of bearing a live born child with Down syndrome is one in 385; at 40 it increases to one in 106; at 45, it is one in thirty" . . . . Another counselor said of advanced maternal age: "It's like

crossing a street with each pregnancy, and when you are older, it's a little easier to be hit by a car. But suppose there is a traffic light. Then, you want to cross on the green. This test puts you back to the green light. Oh, you might still get hit by a crazy hit-and-run driver, but it's not too likely. At the red light [without the test], your age makes you a more likely target for an accident." (Rapp 2000, 68)

Though the heavy use of statistical language lends an air of objectivity and value-neutrality, the last quotation's comparison of some births with an "accident" that ought to be avoided highlights the value-laden nature of the exercise.

Until prenatal genetic testing is universally administered, for technical reasons, testing must be targeted. The main goal of the early part of the counseling session is to teach and guide parents in renarrating their family history in medicalized, "diagnostic" terms. Parents are asked many questions that could be considered surprising or unsettling in normal life: "Have you recently come into contact with cats?" or "Have you taken drugs or had unprotected sex?" or even "Could the child's father be your relative?" Such questions orient the laboratory's investigation of specific anomalies that are linked with these behaviors. In this process the counselor teaches the pregnant woman to reconsider her own biography within the terms of the medical self-understanding, thus constructing a subject who understands herself to carry a certain specifiable "genetic risk" on the basis of this newly constructed narrative of the self.

Rapp observes that there is an inherent confusion shot through these activities of the genetic counselor, who thinks of herself as value-neutral while playing the role of gatekeeper. The biomedical and public health establishments that employ genetic counselors assume that some conceptions are expendable or even burdensome. Genetic counselors simply reproduce this bias in an unreflective manner that "assumes that scientific and medical resources should be placed in the service of prenatal diagnosis and potential elimination of fetuses bearing chromosome problems. In principle, then, counselors are trained to offer a value-charged technology in a value-neutral manner" (Rapp 2000, 59). This lack of self-reflexivity is verified by the surprise of genetic counselors when their advice or even some of the information they have to offer is refused by parents who have decided that abortion is not appropriate for some conditions (Katz Rothman 1986, 256).

It appears, then, that prenatal diagnosis as just described expresses a biomedical account in which prenatal *screening* precedes and is more fundamental than prenatal *care*. At the point that the genetic counselor enters the mix, the prospective parents must learn to evaluate themselves and their growing offspring within the screening framework before making what is termed an "informed" decision for or against the pregnancy. Western society as a whole has learned to "live by the numbers," and the genetic counselor ensures that pregnancy is also understood first in these terms. However, Rapp found that this statistical rationality not only framed the activity of amniocentesis, but barred some from it.

> [I]ronically, the very populations most at risk — less privileged "older" women having more pregnancies with more partners; experiencing more reproductive, perinatal, and infant mortality; and higher death rates throughout their life cycles — may be least likely to live by the numbers precisely because they understand their risks to be spread over a greater territory than chromosome analysis in pregnancy describes. . . . [P]recise biomedical notions of risk are constantly put to empirical challenge by the encompassing and uneven life chances through which women and their supporters encounter them. (Rapp 2000, 312-13)

Much of theological interest appeared in these cases, in which some parents could not or would not evaluate their pregnancies in terms of this metanarrative. Concepts such as value-neutrality, individual choice, risk avoidance, and the authority of expertise are as such not necessarily theologically problematic; but they may become a cocktail that is poisonous to the most vulnerable when they are unreflectively teamed with decisions about whether to eliminate humans perceived to be a social burden. Genetic counselors express the decision of a state, perhaps unwittingly, whose offer to help those mothers most in need of social support has been reduced to the offer of an abortion. This political role is sustained as genetic counselors embrace the role of nondirective (and therefore apolitical) advisor while serving the widespread use of the technologies of elimination. In theological and pastoral terms, the net effect is the loss of attentive empathy and concern for the whole of life while ostensibly in service of the state's interest in minimizing economic cost.

Supererogation in Medical Ethics

In the medical landscape just described, in which some pregnancies are considered too risky for a rational person to seriously consider bringing to term, the concept of supererogation cannot but color the medical professional's sensibilities about the moral nature of parents' decisions to receive pregnancy as a gift rather than as a burden, risk, or threat. My contention is that this is true even when introduced as solely an aspect of professional ethics.

Beauchamp and Childress's *Principles of Biomedical Ethics,* first published in 1979 and now in its fifth edition, has arguably been the most influential account of medical ethics to form the moral aspirations of a generation of medical students in the English-speaking world. Its final chapter turns to describe the ideal medical professional, a moral agent who knows that "what counts most in the moral life is not consistent adherence to principles and rules, but reliable character, moral good sense, and emotional responsiveness" (Beauchamp and Childress 1994, 462). The authors' focus here is on the *virtues* a medical professional must possess, and this suggests that these traits of character cannot — indeed, must not — be confined to professional life alone. Beauchamp and Childress are suggesting here what kind of *people* health-care professionals should be. When medical professionals live the virtues of caring in a consistent way, they build up social capital and come to be seen as "persons of high moral character [who] acquire a reservoir of good will in assessments of the praiseworthiness or blameworthiness of their actions" (Beauchamp and Childress 1994, 464).

I would suggest that the authors need this thick account of the moral aspirations of medical professionals as a buffer against an overly rigid or heartless application of the system of rules and principles that the bulk of their treatment is devoted to explicating. In it they define the virtues of medical professionals: compassion, discernment, trustworthiness, and integrity. Again, it is noteworthy that these virtues are universal: it is inconceivable to think of persons as compassionate, discerning, trustworthy, and possessing moral integrity in their *professional* duties while being callous, undiscerning, untrustworthy characters in the rest of life. Beauchamp and Childress clearly want medical professionals to aspire to be certain kinds of moral agents. The question is whether the moral agents who possess these traits can set them aside when evaluating their patients' decisions.

Here the introduction of the concept of supererogation in the authors' account complicates matters exponentially. They define the concept of supererogation as applying only to specific acts. These acts stand on a spectrum between what is commonly accepted as moral — the ordinary standards of behavior expected of everyone in society — and heroic acts, which can never be demanded of everyone and are not undertaken out of any universal duty. A supererogatory act, according to Beauchamp and Childress, has four features:

> First, a supererogatory act is optional, neither required nor forbidden by common morality standards. Second, supererogatory acts exceed what is expected or demanded by the common morality. Third, supererogatory acts are intentionally undertaken for the welfare of others. Fourth, supererogatory acts are morally good and praiseworthy (not merely undertaken from good intentions). (Beauchamp and Childress 1994, 483)

Let us map this definition of the supererogatory act onto what we have learned about how medical professionals understand prenatal testing. Under the first and second criteria, it is safe to assume that common morality predicates that, all things being equal, it is obligatory to continue an "unaffected" pregnancy. Therefore, to continue an "affected" pregnancy is by definition a decision to go beyond this lower threshold, moving in the direction of a supererogatory or even a heroic act.

The third criterion might also allow a mother's decision to continue an "affected" pregnancy to be interpreted as a decision "intentionally taken for the welfare of others." But as we have seen, many expecting mothers today experience medicine very differently: their choice for the vulnerable is repudiated as serving no one's welfare, not even that of the unborn child. This points to the paternalistic sting in the final criterion, which suggests that for an act to be supererogatory it must be *actually* good and praiseworthy, not just well *intentioned*. In a medical context in which the bearing of a disabled child is explicitly cast in terms of an avoidable accident, the bearing of a disabled child must be understood as a violation of the last criterion of the supererogatory act. If not interpreted as an irrational act because it violates the last criterion, it can, in these terms, be at best considered a decision by idiosyncratic individual parents to go far beyond what the system of prenatal screening assumes parents can reasonably be asked to bear.

Furthermore, Beauchamp and Childress explicitly tie their definition of the threshold between morally obligatory and supererogatory acts in professional life to how much *risk* the subjects take on. It is the level of risk faced as one makes a decision that defines its demands as one of universal moral obligation, or as only an option to be chosen by those inclined to take on a more than average level of risk. The point of the concept of supererogation is to "refrain from holding people to standards that are arduous, risky, and frightening" (Beauchamp and Childress 1994, 487).

In this version of moral medicine, it is the perception of levels of risk, then, that defines an action as supererogatory, or optional and beyond "normal" morality. While presented by the authors only as a criterion within the professional ideal, I have suggested already why these moral aspirations are difficult to confine to strictly professional spheres. Maintaining this separation of professional and private moral aspirations is especially difficult when faced with a pregnant woman who may deny that "perceived risk" is the basic criterion by which carrying a child with a disability is morally defined. When we bring this self-understanding together with the mechanisms of prenatal testing that systematically accentuate certain narrow aspects of the riskiness of pregnancy, we can see some of the reasons why human vulnerability appears to medical professionals in this context as something to be avoided. In this light, the concept of supererogation functions to heighten the extant social stereotypes within which women who wish to accept the most vulnerable in their wombs are portrayed as, at best, making a heroic decision, at worst, an immoral one.

The Theological Critique of Supererogation

While there may be a historical connection between medieval and modern concepts of supererogation, it may be wiser not to insist on a direct line of descent, because there is at least one important dis-analogy, which appears in how Kant defined the concept. Kant not only reintroduced the concept into modern moral discourse, but his definition of the term also shapes most modern usage, including that of Beauchamp and Childress. Kant's reasons for seeking a concept to distinguish between the duties owed to all people from those owed only to some under special circumstances, draws on a concept of morality as transtemporal and exceptionless because based on universal reason. In the medieval tradition, however, "supererogation" was primarily used as an *ecclesial* distinction, distinguishing between higher and lower paths of virtue. But the critical confluence between the two thought systems is the presupposition that there is a "regular" duty to the neighbor and a "special" duty not incumbent on everyone. In any case, the ethics of Kantian neo-Protestantism attempted to recover a distinction with this function, and thus returned to this term.

With regard to this presupposition, Calvin expresses the protest of the magisterial Reformation to any bifurcation of moral claims in this manner: "Since we are unduly inclined to hypocrisy, this palliative ought by no means be added to soothe our sluggish consciences" (Calvin 1960, 2.8.58). Such disavowals were to have a long history in Protestant theology, as marked by its anathematization in the Anglican Thirty-Nine Articles (Art. 14): "The works of supererogation cannot be taught without arrogance and impiety" (O'Donovan 1986, Appendix I). Indeed, it is not going too far to say that the Reformation began with exactly this worry about the notion of a "higher way" on which a long and developed theological account of supererogation and vocation had rested. Such moral exception clauses appeared to cut the vital cord of transformative faith to yield a culturally conservative and conformist Christianity (Luther 1966, 17-33; 1957b, 44-45).

Luther was reacting at a fundamental and theological level against a medieval development of a firm distinction between following both Christ's commands (charity, understood through the cardinal virtues) and his more strenuous counsels (poverty, chastity, and obedience). This distinction was mapped onto the monastic-laity distinction, with the nomenclature of "vocation" linked to the higher way, as in Aquinas's *Summa Theologica* (Aquinas 1906, 2a, 2ae, 185.6). In the theologies of the Reformation, the concept of vocation was decisively reformulated and applied both to activities as apparently different as the work of the priesthood, trade, parenthood, and government. This leveling or sacralization of all spheres of human work has had a deep and enduring effect on the ways moderns conceive their lives and work, and, as I have tried to show, has deeply problematized attempts such as those of Beauchamp and Childress, which assume that sharp distinctions can be drawn between "personal" and "professional" ethics (Taylor 1989, part III).

The English term "supererogation" marks its direct descent from theological usage in being a derivation of the Latin *erogare* (meaning "to pay or expend") as it prominently appears in the (Latin) Vulgate in Jesus' parable of the Good Samaritan. The Samaritan, having rescued the injured neighbor, cares for him, takes him to an inn, tells the proprietor to care for him, and promises to reimburse his expenses, as it says in Luke 10:35, "and whatever you spend besides" *(quodcumque supererogaveris)*. Zacchaeus's superabundant restitution (Luke 19:8-9) and Paul's using his own funds to support his ministry (Acts 20:34; 1 Thess. 3:8-9) also serve as paradigmatic examples of supererogation. Whereas Thomas Aquinas and others had solidified the distinction between commands and counsels in a highly technical manner (*Summa Theologica*, 1a2ae 108.2-4), Luther argued that we could in truth obey neither Christ's counsels nor his commands, and so are constantly thrown back on grace and into love of the neighbor without hesitation or moral hairsplitting — completely without reserve (Luther 1957a, 348; 1966, 33).

Luther bequeathed to evangelical ethics a sensitivity to the difference between embarking on projects of moral calculation and justification, yielding a two-tier morality, and the single-tier morality of attentiveness to the neighbor. The Lutheran doctrine of spontaneous good works is, among other things, an insistence that it was no accident that Jesus answered the question about what it means to love one's neighbor with the story of the Good Samaritan. With this story Jesus revalues the Pharisee's question, "Who, then, is my neighbor?" He refuses his interlocutor's assumption that morality begins with trying to define the other "out there" to whom empathy and solicitude is due. His question is wholly different: Who *turned out* to have been a neighbor? Faithfulness here appears as a transformed consciousness in which one's own self-interest is wholly tied to the well-being of the other. Jesus thus suggests the moral force of a specific form of attentiveness to others. Jesus is depicted in the Gospels as trying to inflame this kind of attentiveness in his hearers.

In terms of this attentiveness to the neighbor, the spontaneous responsiveness of the Good Samaritan turns out not to be "irrational" or "unpredictable," but a very practical rationality. Jesus asks us to become people whose investigation of human fragility does not begin by our distancing of ourselves from others as "subjects," but by training ourselves to respond without excuse and without forethought to existing human need. I take this spontaneity to be the *premise* out of which a laboriously cultivated way of life such as L'Arche can emerge. As Jean Vanier himself puts it, L'Arche is a school for relationships, a community where people can discover the fecundity of divine love through attentiveness to others. To discover such spontaneity is a gift of the Spirit that cannot be ensured or legislated by any law, but begins in the prayer that requests it. Such love, as Jesus' parable suggests, requires *conversion*, not simply information or education.

This answer has appeared to most modern Christian moralists as an insufficiently broad account of the foundations of Christian ethics. But that is to overlook the fact that the parable of the Good Samaritan also implies that a steady emphasis on the occasional and gratuitous nature of Christian responsiveness is not opposed to more hardheaded institutional thinking (*pace* Reinhold Niebuhr 1932), but in fact demands it (Ulrich 2005, 109). The Good Samaritan, after all, took his neighbor to an inn for care. Institutions are not the opposite of spontaneity; institutions may aim at or thwart our being turned out of ourselves and toward others. An inn, as a meeting of economic, political, and interpersonal cultures, may be a better or worse place for the Good Samaritan to leave his ward. This insight grounds the cultural criticism of Christian ethics, which is at every point a social ethic.

This understanding of neighbor love combines with Christian commitments to the good of noncoercion in political affairs to yield a refusal of any suggestion that such Spirit-enabled spontaneity can be imposed on all of society. A properly Christian political ethic will thus seek social structures that can protect and promote the space for spontaneous attentiveness to occur, even though the focus on Christlike attentiveness to the neighbor cannot be reduced to or translated into the language of secular rationality. Christians living in communities such as L'Arche can thus be nothing more than witness, one that has *political* benefits that Christians have a duty to offer to a secular political society that cannot conceive it on its own terms (Wannenwetsch 2004, chap. 8).[2] Such a witness stands as a word from outside and above us about the necessity of listening to the voices of those who challenge our presuppositions by wishing to bear and live with the most vulnerable of humans.

References

Aquinas. 1906. *Summa theologica of St. Thomas Aquinas,* trans. Fathers of the English Dominican Province. London: Burns, Oates and Washbourne.

Beauchamp, T. L., and J. Childress. 1994. *Principles of biomedical ethics.* Oxford: Oxford University Press.

Brock, B., W. Dörfler, and H. Ulrich. 2007. Genetics, conversation and conversion: A discourse at the interface of molecular biology and Christian ethics. In *Theology, disability and the new genetics: Why science needs the church,* ed. J. Swinton and B. Brock). London: T. & T. Clark.

Calvin, J. 1960. *Institutes of the Christian religion.* Ed. John McNeill. Trans. Ford

---

2. Wannenwetsch is commenting on the influential claim to this effect of Karl Barth in "The Christian Community and the Civil Community," sec. 14.

Lewis Battles. The Library of Christian Classics, vols. 21-22. Philadelphia: Westminster.

Katz Rothman, B. 1986. *The tentative pregnancy: Prenatal diagnosis and the future of motherhood*. New York: Penguin Books.

Luther, M. 1957a. The freedom of a Christian. In *Luther's Works: American Edition*, ed. Harold J. Grimm and Helmut T. Lehmann, vol. 31. Philadelphia: Fortress.

————. 1957b. Ninety-five Theses. In *Luther's Works: American Edition*, ed. Harold J. Grimm and Helmut T. Lehmann, vol. 31. Philadelphia: Fortress.

————. 1966. Treatise on good works, 1520. In *Luther's Works: American Edition*, ed. James Atkinson and Helmut T. Lehmann, vol. 44. Philadelphia: Fortress.

Niebuhr, Reinhold. 1932. *Moral man and immoral society: A study in ehtics and politics*. New York: Scribner's.

O'Donovan, O. 1986. *The Thirty Nine Articles: A conversation with Tudor Christianity*. Exeter, UK: Paternoster.

Rapp, R. 2000. *Testing women, testing the fetus: The social impact of amniocentesis in America*. New York: Routledge.

Tankard Reist, M. 2006. *Defiant birth: Women who resist medical eugenics*. North Melbourne: Spinifex.

Taylor, C. *Sources of the self: The making of the modern identity*. Part III: The affirmation of ordinary life. Cambridge, MA: Harvard University Press.

Ulrich, Hans. 2005. *Wie geschöpfe Leben: Konturen evangelischer Ethik*. Münster: Lit Verlag.

Wannenwetsch, Bernd. 2004. *Ethics for Christian citizens*. Trans Margaret Kohl. Oxford: Oxford University Press.

Chapter Eleven

Known by God

John Swinton

Introduction

Two weeks ago I received this email from a friend who is a worship leader in my church:

> Hi John,
>
> The worship band from our church has been invited into some Special Needs schools, which is great fun. I started off doing schools work in a severe special needs school years ago and I think we saw kids who lacked the intellectual ability to understand God meet with him in worship. Of course music can be very powerful and perhaps it was more so for those guys, but often staff members would point out different kids who responded in greater ways when we did worship than when other people came and did music with them. The response I have occasionally heard when I've mentioned that to people [Evangelical Christians] is that we can only worship what we know, or that worship only comes as a response to a revelation. Can you give me an impressive sounding answer to come back with?
>
> Peace
> *James*

Reading this reminded me of various incidents in my life when I have encountered similar modes of theology and practice that implicitly or explicitly excluded people with profound intellectual disabilities. In my former role as a nurse working with people who have intellectual disabilities, and then later as a mental-health chaplain, I constantly encountered attitudes and assumptions that seemed to exclude people with profound learning disabilities from having a meaningful relationship with God. I remember how I felt when I was writing my undergraduate thesis on how Christian communities should offer care and friendship to people with profound intellectual disabilities. I had just made the transition from nursing to theology, and I was excited and filled with anticipation about how the two might come together. However, as I read through some of the literature, I began to see that my excitement and anticipation may have been misplaced. The more I read, the more I realized that there was a dangerous lack of clarity about precisely what it means to claim that one knows God and has an intimate relationship with God, a lack of clarity that had profound implications for how the church understands and responds to people whom we have chosen to label "profoundly intellectually disabled." A good example of the difficulties can be summed up in a quotation from an essay by nurse-educator Peter Birchenall. Reflecting on the role of community and church in caring for people with intellectual disabilities, Birchenall observes:

> [P]eople with a profound mental handicap [*sic*] possess a limited ability to reason at the complex level, and are therefore not able to work through any doubts and develop any sort of faith. (Birchenall and Birchenall 1986, 150).

In a later article he says:

> Severely mentally handicapped people are denied the very substance of a rational productive existence, and are confined to a life of almost total dependence on others for even their most basic needs. Such an existence gives no real opportunity for inner spiritual growth, or the nourishment of the human spirit, both of which are important when coming to terms with the meaning of Christianity. It gives no real opportunity to experience the joy of seeking a lifetime relationship with the Almighty, because the concepts involved are complicated and require a level of awareness which the profoundly mentally handicapped do not have. (Birchenall 1987, 75).

The assumption here seems to be that, in order to find joy in one's relationship with God, one has to understand God via one's intellect and to be able to articulate this knowledge in a way that reveals, in quite particular and selective ways, one's conscious awareness of God. The emphasis seems to be on knowing *about* God rather than being known by God. The concept of faith seems to relate primarily and perhaps exclusively to forms of relating that are based on the intellect. The principles of rationality are inseparably linked with knowledge of God and spiritual growth in a way that assumes a) that knowing God is the result of an action based in a particular human capability, and b) that only some human beings have that capability and are therefore able to carry out that action. To know God is to understand who God is at an intellectual level. Such a position automatically excludes those who do not appear to have such capacities.

Sadly, church communities are not exempt from such unfortunate assumptions. At a C.A.S.P.E.N. conference in 1991,[1] I spoke with a Church of Scotland minister whose daughter has Down syndrome. She was a member of the Church of Scotland, and she was a regular attender and participant in worship. He told me that, while in Aberdeen five years earlier, he and his wife and daughter had gone to a city center Church of Scotland for communion. The cup was passed round, but when it reached the handicapped woman, the minister who was administering communion refused to allow her to participate in the Eucharist. His reason was that he did not believe that she had the intellectual capability to understand and meaningfully participate in the sacrament. From his theological standpoint, the girl's participation would risk demeaning or even invalidating the sacrament.[2] It is easy to imagine the humiliation and exclusion the family felt that day.

"But surely," one might say, "these stories are twenty years old! We understand disability differently today. We no longer think in those ways!"

---

1. C.A.S.P.E.N. is a program initiated by the Church of Scotland's research and development department. Its intention is to produce resource material and offer training for ministers that will enable them to prepare people with special needs for church membership and participation in the sacraments.

2. It is interesting to reflect on 1 Cor. 11: 27-32 in the light of such experiences: "So then, whoever eats the bread or drinks the cup of the Lord in an unworthy manner will be guilty of sinning against the body and blood of the Lord. [All] ought to examine themselves before they eat of the bread and drink of the cup. For those who eat and drink without discerning the body of Christ eat and drink judgment on themselves. That is why many among you are weak and sick, and a number of you have fallen asleep. But if we were more discerning with regard to ourselves, we would not come under such judgment. Nevertheless, when we are judged in this way by the Lord, we are being disciplined so that we will not be finally condemned with the world" (NIV).

However, the vignette with which I opened this chapter, combined with recent high-profile cases of the sacramental exclusion of people with intellectual disabilities within the Christian church, would indicate that what was true then is much truer today than we might be comfortable in admitting. These examples raise quite sharply some of the issues that I want to address in this chapter (see also Webb-Mitchell 1996; Swinton 1999). In responding to these issues, I wish to draw on aspects of two Christian theological traditions, the apophatic tradition and the theology of liberation. Some thoughtful reflections on the insights that these traditions bring to the current discussion will allow us to develop a positive theology *with* people whose life experiences include profound intellectual disabilities.

Profound and Complex Intellectual Disability

From the outset it will be helpful for me to be clear as to precisely what kind of disability I am talking about. I am not talking about people with so-called moderate intellectual disabilities. Those with this life experience can, given the appropriate support and encouragement, articulate their own spiritual needs and participate within Christian communities in ways that do not raise the issues I have highlighted thus far. My focus in this chapter is on people with profound and complex intellectual disabilities. For the purposes of this chapter, I will use the term "profound and complex intellectual disability" to refer to people who have a severe disability that includes significant intellectual and/or cognitive impairment, severe communication difficulties, and high support needs. The key thing to acknowledge here is that, for many people with this life experience, language is not their primary means of communication. Accordingly, their modes of communicating, learning, and relating are not shaped by the ability to conceptualize the objects of their encounters and articulate this in language. It is this kind of life experience that raises the sorts of questions about faith, worship, and knowledge of God that are highlighted in the opening sections of this essay.

Knowing or Being Known?

It seems to me that the underlying problem with the kinds of understandings and assumptions highlighted thus far is that the theological dynamic is fundamentally misdirected. At a very basic level, the assumption that our relationship with God is in any way dependant on the presence or absence of human capabilities is a theological mistake. In Ephesians 2:8-9, the apostle Paul makes this statement about the means of our salvation: "For it is by grace you have been saved, through faith — and this not from yourselves, it is the gift of God — not by works, so that no one can boast." Faith itself is not a human achievement but a grace-full gift. Therefore, unless we take a hypercognitive perspective on what it means to be "sure of what we hope for and certain of what we do not see," we find ourselves open to interesting "new" possibilities.

If we switch to a perspective that focuses on a relationship with God that is based on receiving, Birchenall's argument soon begins to come apart. What would rule out the possibility that "the Almighty" might seek a lifetime relationship with the profoundly disabled person quite apart from that person's ability to intellectualize and/or articulate that relationship? If worship is "a response to a revelation," then clearly it is a gift of the Spirit and not a work of the intellect. Likewise, if the sacraments are, as Calvin put it, visible signs of an invisible grace, then they are not things that we do, but grace-full actions of the Holy Spirit within which we are called to receive the gifts that God desires to give to us (Migliore 2004, 280). If the theological dynamic begins and ends in divine grace and human reception, then the situation of people with profound intellectual disabilities begins to look quite different. We will need to do some deeper reflection before we can make this point convincingly. For the present, suffice it to note that, viewed in this way, the issue is not really one of intellect versus experience, but activism versus reception.

The Contemplative Tradition

One way in which we can begin to develop our understanding about these issues is by turning to the contemplative tradition. At heart, the contemplative tradition seeks ways in which we can learn what it means to love God fully in all things — in all ways and at all times. This tradition does not perceive one's relationship with God primarily as an act of the intellect, though it certainly includes that. The contemplatives see the intellect as important; however, that importance is significantly different from the ways in which the narrators who opened this chapter perceived it. Much of what the contemplatives try to achieve relates to the slightly paradoxical idea of using the intellect to move beyond the intellect to allow contemplatives to experience a relationship within which they encounter God's love in intense ways. As Thomas Merton puts it, the contemplative seeks to "know by 'unknowing.' Or, better, we know *beyond* all knowing or 'unknowing'" (Merton 2002, 13). The heart of the contemplative's task is to learn what it means not simply to love God, but to love God only for God's sake; not for what she wants from God and not for what she can give to God; indeed, not even for what she hopes God will do in the future. Her task is to learn to love God simply for God's sake. Bernard of Clairvaux puts it this way:

> You ask me, "Why should God be loved?" I answer: the reason for loving God is God himself. And why should God be loved for his own sake? Simply because no one could be more justly loved than God, no one deserves our love more. Some may question if God deserves our love or if they might have something to gain from loving him. The answer to both questions is yes, but I find no other worthy reason for loving him except himself.[3]

The contemplative seeks to purge herself from the bonds of the intellect that often prevent her from loving God in order that she can enter into a state of loving God that is pure and concentrated. Her joy is found not in intellectual knowledge about God but in a form of loving experience that is infused into her by the Holy Spirit. And here we find a vital point for current purposes. While her rigorous spiritual discipline may be designed to enable her to come closer to God, in reality it is not her actions that achieve this task but the actions of God through the work of the Holy Spirit. Her participation is, I am sure, meaningful in God's eyes, but the spiritual dynamic is always one of receiving and not one of giving or attaining through human effort or ability. Thomas Merton puts it this way: "Contemplation is a supernatural love and knowledge of God, simple and obscure, infused by him into the summit of the soul, giving it a direct and experimental contact with him" (Merton 1995, 98). "It is a gift of God that absolutely transcends all the natural capacities of the soul and which no man can acquire by any effort of his own" (Merton 1995, 98). In this way the contemplative tradition brings us clearly and gently into the knowledge that all we have is gift, and that no matter how hard we strive to get closer to God, in the end it is he who comes to us and not the other way around.

The Impossibility of Knowing God

There are various strands within the contemplative tradition.[3] Here I want to focus on one strand: the *apophatic* tradition (from the Greek *apophasis:* "denial, negation"). Apophatic theology refuses to assign attributes to God; rather, it argues that all names attributed to God and all of our intellectual conceptualizations of God are inevitably inadequate. Because it so transcends creation, God's reality cannot be described or captured by the human intellect or expressed in human language. The anonymous writer of *The Cloud of Unknowing* says:

> For the love of God, therefore, be careful in this work and never strain your mind or imagination, for truly you will not succeed in this way. Leave these faculties at peace.
>
> It is God, and he alone, who can fully satisfy the hunger and longing of our spirit which transformed by his redeeming grace is enabled to embrace him by love. He whom neither men nor angels can grasp by knowledge can be embraced by love. For the intellect of both men and angels is too small to comprehend God as he is in himself. (Johnston 2005, 44, 42)

Here we find another piece of the emerging picture of the movement from act to gift. Only God satisfies "the hunger and longing of our spirit," which his grace transforms so that it may be enabled to embrace him. It is as we are embraced by God's love that we find ourselves able to embrace God in love. Our part in this divine movement of grace-full love is one of response; however, any response in whatever form it might take is always contingent on the gracious gift that the Holy Spirit brings to the encounter. When we begin to understand the dynamics of the movement of God to human beings, our imaginations are no longer bound by the limits of our reason, or indeed any other faculty. We are freed to love.

> Thought cannot comprehend God. And so, I prefer to abandon all I can know, choosing rather to love him whom I cannot know. Though we

3. Thomas Merton has noted two lines of contemplation within the tradition: a contemplation of light (Origen, Augustine, Saint Bernard) and a contemplation of darkness (Gregory of Nyssa, Pseudo-Dionysius, and Saint John of the Cross). He argues that the difference between these two schools is in the language each uses to describe mystical union rather than the nature of the experience described. Merton, *The Ascent to Truth* (New York: Harcourt, Brace, 1951), pp. 25-29, 292-93.

cannot know him we can love him. By love he may be touched and embraced, never by thought. (Johnston 2005, 44)

The human encounter with God sits in that strange space between knowing and not knowing: revelation and hiddenness. The recognition of the great mystery of God and the deep sense of unknowability does not mean that we can know nothing of God, only that what we know is always tentative and partial.[4]

God cannot be possessed or his love bound inextricably to any human faculty. God is known as he reveals himself in whatever way he desires:

Of course, it is impossible in this life to see and possess God fully but, with his grace and in his own time, it is possible to taste something of him as he is in himself. . . . [L]et God awaken your longing and draw you to himself . . . while you strive with the help of his grace to forget everything else. (Johnston 2005, 52)

We can know God, but all that we know is what God gives us. Through God's grace and in the power of the Holy Spirit it is possible to know some things about God, but only as God reveals them to us as we learn to let go of all things that distract us from loving God. Love, not the intellect, is the key to knowing God. Each of us in different ways can grasp God through our love.

No one can fully comprehend the uncreated God with his knowledge, but each one, in a different way, can grasp him fully through love. Truly this is the unending miracle of love: that one loving person, through his love, can embrace God, whose being fills and transcends the entire creation. (Johnston 2005, 42)

The God who is Spirit and who is truth (John 4:20-24) comes to us in our helplessness and reveals something of himself in the midst of our cloud of unknowing. The revelation cannot be captured in human language or understood via human intellect and reason. It is experienced in love and revealed in God's loving, graceful gestures toward human beings and the hu-

---

4. There are, of course, various traditions within "the apophatic tradition," something that is not always acknowledged by its critics. For example, Colin Gunton, in his trenchant critique of the apophatic tradition, speaks of "the tradition" as if it were monolithic. His argument that apophatic theology doesn't take revelation and Christology seriously applies to some writers but certainly not to others. Cf., e.g., St. John of the Cross. Gunton, *Act and Being: Toward a Theology of the Divine Attributes* (London: SCM Press, 2002).

man responses to that love. The contemplative tradition thus moves us away from a concentration on the intellect to a focus on God's gift of love, which he gives to all people (John 1:4) and to which people respond according to the lives they have been given. It may be that our encounters with people whose life experiences include profound and complex needs remind us of truths that are often forgotten in a culture that prizes human activism and progress above most things.

Knowing God in Social Practices: Insights from Theologies of Liberation

But one might still ask some probing questions: How can someone love God when a person doesn't know who God is? Even if we accept that God's revelation is a gift, don't we certainly need some understanding of who the giver is before we can effectively appropriate the gift and learn to love the giver? Further, while we of course recognize that we only see God, as we do all things, through a dark veil (1 Cor. 1:13), isn't Jesus surely the revelation of God? Paradoxically, God is unknowable, but he is knowable through Jesus — isn't he?

There is clearly a tension here between God's unknowability and his revelation in Jesus. This, in turn, raises the question of precisely what it means to know or be known by Jesus. I propose that people with profound and complex intellectual disabilities (as with all people) come to know Jesus as they come to know those who seek to offer them care, support, and above all, friendship. In line with my previous points, this knowledge of God is revealed through the Holy Spirit, but it is revealed as the Holy Spirit is embodied in faithful people.

Jose Miranda, speaking from within the liberation theology tradition, makes an interesting point here:

> To know Jahweh is to achieve justice for the poor. . . . The God who does not allow himself to be objectified, because only in the immediate command of conscience is he God, clearly specifies that he is knowable exclusively in the cry of the poor and the weak who seek justice. (Miranda 1977, 94-97)

Miranda's point is that God does not reveal himself in abstract concepts but primarily in actions aimed at enabling justice and liberation for the poor. God is known only as we participate in such actions. Miranda raises an important point, though one might want to argue that his position is overstated and slightly reductionist. We certainly meet God in actions that are aimed at justice and liberation for the poor, but that is not the only place where we learn what it means to know God. Nevertheless, his central point is sensitizing: our knowledge of God always comes to us in some form of embodied human action and relationship. We meet God in actions that in turn reveal God's justice and love. It is important to notice what this implies. The kind of theology highlighted in the introduction to this chapter assumes the epistemological and soteriological priority of knowing *about* God. However, "knowing about" God presupposes absence: that is, God does not have to be present and active for one to know about God. Knowing as participation, on the other hand, implies presence. God is not a concept but a living encounter. There is an inseparable unity between loving actions and knowing God.[5] But that unity is much more than mere cause and effect: I love God; therefore, I act in particular ways. There is a real sense in Scripture that God is present *within* particular forms of social action, and that it is as we participate in these actions that we encounter and learn to know and to love God. This is what Miranda raises our consciousness to.

God's intimate identification with and presence within particular individuals or groups is found throughout Scripture with respect to God's relationship with the poor and those who are outcast.[6] In Jeremiah 22:16 we find this text: "'He judged the cause of the poor and the needy; then it was well. Is not this to know me?' says the Lord." This is a fascinating proposition. Taken in its wider context, the text speaks about good and bad kings and offers Josiah as a model of a good king because he cared for the poor and the needy. The similarity between this text and Miranda's statement is tantalizing. Walter Brueggemann observes:

> This is an extraordinary text which shows how Yahweh is understood in terms of a social practice. Note well, the text does not say that if one takes care of the poor and needy, then one will get to know Yahweh. Nor does the text say that, if one knows Yahweh, then one will take care of the poor and needy. The two elements are not sequential nor are they

---

5. "Everyone who loves is born of God and knows God. Whoever does not love does not know God, because God is love" (1 John 4:7b-8).

6. The entire book of James is really a commentary on this statement.

related as cause and effect. Rather, the two phrases are synonymous. Caring for the poor and the needy is equivalent to knowing Yahweh. That is who Yahweh is and how Yahweh is known. Yahweh is indeed a mode of social practice and a form of social relation. (Brueggemann 2001, 12)

This has important implications for the issues I am exploring in this essay. It is as we offer care, support, and friendship to people with profound intellectual disabilities that we come to know and to love God. It is as people with profound intellectual disabilities encounter their friends in loving relationships that the unarticulated (and unarticulable?) stirrings of the Holy Spirit become embodied and tangible.[7] However, it is important not to interpret my argument as turning people with profound intellectual disabilities into passive objects of Christian charity. My intention is quite the opposite. A reflection on Matthew 25 will help make this point clear.

Knowing God in Social Practices

In Matthew 25:35-40, Jesus reflects on the final judgment and the relationship of God to those whom the world considers to be strangers. On the last day, Jesus will sit on the seat of judgment and separate those who were for him in this life from those who were against him, the sheep to the right and the goats to the left. In this passage Jesus clearly identifies himself as the *xenos,* the stranger, the one whom many refused to befriend. Jesus calls his people to recognize the stranger as the one whom they are obliged to care for and protect. Those who offer hospitality and friendship toward the stranger will be welcomed into the kingdom of heaven; those who fail to offer such hospitality to the *xenos* will depart from the presence of the Lord into everlasting fire (Matt. 25:41-46). In offering hospitality toward strangers we encounter Jesus.

It is important to note that in this passage Jesus does not simply entreat people to pursue acts of charity toward the stranger (i.e., "if you know me, then you will act in this way"). The relationship between Jesus

---

7. Romans 8:26: "In the same way, the Spirit helps us in our weakness. We do not know what we ought to pray for, but the Spirit himself intercedes for us with groans that words cannot express."

and "the stranger" seems to be quite different. Jesus is not simply *with* the poor and the oppressed; in a very real sense, he is *in* the poor and the oppressed — "the stranger." Jesus declares quite clearly that acts of charity and friendship toward strangers are in fact gestures of love *toward himself.* In calling his disciples to perform radical acts of hospitality and to recognize their theological significance, Jesus places "strangers" under divine protection and places his followers under divine obligation to offer hospitality to them. The implications of such a suggestion for offering care and support to people with profound and complex intellectual disabilities — people who are clearly marked as strangers in an intellectually oriented culture such as ours — are not difficult to imagine.

But there is more to this passage. There is much debate about precisely to whom Jesus addressed this passage. Was it a general statement to all people? Was it simply to his disciples? There is no doubt that, at a minimum, it was for his disciples. This has crucial implications for Christian caregivers and for those with profound and complex intellectual disabilities who are involved within Christian communities. Jesus is in those to whom we seek to offer care; but he is also within those who offer care in the name of Jesus. "We" — caregiver and cared with — are the poor. Those disciples who seek to offer Christian care to people with profound and complex intellectual disabilities very quickly discover that the people they assume they should be caring for begin to minister to the Jesus within them. Very soon the idea of caring *for* is shifted into the cadence of caring *with.* The rhythm of Christian care begins with being ministered to by Jesus in the "stranger." As Jesus ministers to us, so we minister to him. It is as we recognize the poverty of our own spirits and learn to accept the ministry of Jesus as it comes to us in the stranger that we all discover that God's actions precede our loving acts of response. It's all gift.

Knowledge of God for both caregiver and cared-for is thus seen to emerge from and become embodied within the social practices that comprise the essence of their loving encounter. Understood in this way, the gentle gestures of love — laughter, touch, embrace, friendship, encounter — take on the shape of God and enable each participant to encounter the other in ways that embody the knowledge of God and facilitate modes of revelation that are inspired by the Spirit and embraced and lived out by the community-of-the-friends-of-Jesus. In faith, all participants learn what it means to be sure of what they hope for and secure in what they cannot see.

Conclusion

In conclusion, it has become clear that knowledge of God has to do primarily with participation in and response to God. It is first and foremost a gift of the Spirit. God is, in a very real sense, unknowable apart from what God chooses to reveal to human beings. Our dependence on God is an aspect of life for all people, but the issue is brought into sharp focus as we reflect on the lives of people with profound and complex intellectual disabilities. God reveals himself in Scripture, but also within the love that is manifested within the community-of-the-friends-of-Jesus. People with profound and complex intellectual disabilities come to know the character of God as they encounter God in relationships with others. Knowledge of God comes through the Holy Spirit, and it is as we receive this knowledge that we learn what it means to embody knowing God in our relationships and our communities. As the apostle John puts it: "No one has ever seen God; if we love one another, God lives in us, and his love is perfected in us" (1 John 4:12). If we take these theological reflections seriously, we will soon discover a whole new way of caring with people who have profound intellectual disabilities, and in so doing we will encounter a mode of discipleship that is both faithful and transformative.

References

Bernard of Clairvaux. *On the Love of God.* Christian Classics Ethereal Library: http://www.ccel.org/ (accessed Dec. 14, 2006).

Birchenall, P., and M. Birchenall. 1986. Caring for mentally handicapped people: The community and the church. *The Professional Nurse* 1 (6): 148-50.

Brueggemann, W. 2001. The practice of homefullness. *Church and Society* May/June: 12.

Gunton, C. 2002. *Act and being: Toward a theology of the divine attributes.* London: SCM.

Johnston, W., ed. 2005. *The cloud of unknowing and the book of privy counseling.* New York: Random House.

Merton, T. 1951. *The ascent to truth.* New York: Harcourt, Brace.

———. 1995. *Spiritual direction and meditation and what is contemplation.* Hertfordshire: Anthony Clarke.

———. 2002. *New seeds of contemplation.* London: Continuum.

Migliore, D. 2004. *Faith seeking understanding: An introduction to Christian theology.* 2nd ed. Grand Rapids: Eerdmans.

Miranda, J. 1977. *Marx and the Bible: A critique of the philosophy of oppression.* London: SCM.

Swinton, J. 1999. *A space to listen: The spiritual lives of people with learning disabilities.* London: Mental Health Foundation.

Web-Mitchell, B. 1996. *Dancing with disabilities: Opening the church to all God's children.* Cleveland: United Church Press/Pilgrim Press.

Chapter Twelve

Watch the Lilies of the Field:
Theological Reflections on Profound
Disability and Time

HANS S. REINDERS

*Father in heaven! From you come only good and perfect gifts. It must
also be beneficial to comply with the counsel and teaching of whomever
you have appointed as a teacher of human beings, as a counselor to the
worried.*

Søren Kierkegaard

The Question

What, if anything, can we learn from profoundly disabled human beings?
The question is not at all self-evident, given the general features of a profoundly disabled human life. Roughly, the notion of a profoundly disabled
life indicates the life of someone who exists without having a notion of
herself as a human being, without language, and without plans and projects. The way people with profound disabilities are connected to the world
is through their senses, which is why their existence has been compared
frequently with that of animal life. One way this comparison is articulated
is to say that, not unlike the animals, human beings with profound disabilities do not know time: they live in the eternal here and now, not by choice
but by necessity. Again, what, if anything, can we possibly learn from people living this kind of life?

I suggest that we approach this question by thinking about the experience of time. Since people with profound disabilities live without any
awareness of time, they also do not have a sense of their own past, nor do

they have hopes for their own future. The reason is that both remembrance and expectation presuppose representation, which is a mental activity that we cannot ascribe to profoundly disabled human beings, at least not insofar as representation presupposes language. Beyond the absence of language, or any other means of symbolic communication, we simply have no indication that we can ascribe memories and hopes — rather than "mere" desires — to a profoundly disabled human being.

These remarks explain a great deal of why their kind of life appears to be alien to most other people. They do not know "now" as distinct from "then"; nor is there a sense of days gone by or days to come. Therefore, there are no representations of themselves in different times and places — again, insofar as we can tell. Given the fundamental place the experience of time takes in our own lives, it is very hard to imagine what it is to live without that experience. It is probably because of this difficulty that the humanity of profoundly disabled human beings appears doubtful to some. Being without expectations and hopes for one's own future, one cannot live a truly human life, according to some philosophers (e.g., Harris 1985; but see Reinders 2007). Indeed, once we think about it, many human experiences presuppose the experience of time, such as the experience of acting for a purpose.

Time and Meaning

In this essay I will refer to the experience of time that is familiar to most of us as "subjective time." Subjective time means having a sense of living now between past and future. Having a sense of living between past and future is deemed of crucial importance, particularly in Western culture. The reason is that subjective time structures our activities. Subjective time is the vehicle of human agency. People in our culture tend to think about their daily lives primarily in terms of having things to do. We schedule our time, carry a personal calendar, make plans, and set appointments. These behaviors are connected with a will to achieve whatever goals we have set for ourselves, as well as with our worries when we fail. Without subjective time, those are all incomprehensible states of mind. By the same token, the absence of subjective time cannot but indicate how alien the lives must be of those that are lacking it. They live in an eternal here and now.[1]

---

1. There is the view that living in the eternal here and now is the true condition of hu-

The notion of human agency, acting for a purpose, is linked to the notion of meaning, at least in Western culture. Images of successful lives that are transmitted by popular media send the message that the meaning of life is what we ourselves make of it, thus the unceasing admiration in this culture for the "self-made man." "Making it" is a culturally calibrated expression that indicates the power of achievement: "If you can make it there, you can make it anywhere." The flip side of this cultural image is inevitably that living a life without achievements must appear as empty. Time is void of meaning, unless it is filled by our own action. Because the meaning of time is what we make of it, subjective time must be of crucial importance in our lives.

I take the truth of these reflections to be self-evident for most people in our modern culture. In the eyes of some, perhaps many, it even appears as an oppressive truth, which is why we are urged to take a break and forget about being busy and being consumed with time.[2] It would be hard to explain the reason for such urgings and recommendations, however, if it were not for a general belief that purposive action is what creates meaning in the first place. What we need to be liberated from, apparently, is the idea that time needs to be "filled" with our own projects. Instead, what we need to accept, it seems, is that time inevitably is empty. There would be no point in spreading this countercultural message, I am suggesting, if many people in our culture would not believe that a successful life depends on the ability to create a meaningful life for ourselves.

Living in God's Time

Underlying the cultural belief that human beings create meaning by pursuing their own projects, then, is the assumption of empty time. My aim

---

man happiness, which is usually connected with the Buddhist notion of "selflessness" as the state of bliss that is ascribed to the *bodhisattva* becoming *buddha*. According to this notion, the eternal here and now equals timelessness, while existing in timelessness equals the state of *anatman*, or "nonself." From this perspective, the lives of people living in that state appear as an exemplary state of being. But a discussion of the Buddhist perspective on selflessness must wait till some other time. In this essay I will pursue a Christian understanding of living in the eternal here and now as living in God's time, which is not timelessness.

2. One only needs to conduct a search on the Web for "eternal here and now" to find numerous recommendations by self-styled Buddhists and other gurus suggesting that "time" is a closed circle that the wise know how to transcend.

in this essay is to reflect on this state of affairs theologically. Therefore, I will ask what it means to say that, as human beings, we live in God's time. "Living in God's time" is an expression that I deliberately use to oppose and to undermine the assumption of empty time. The most basic reason is that — at least from the perspective of Jews, Muslims, and Christians — if God is the creator of the universe, then time cannot be empty. Consequently, there is no need to fill time with our own projects, because basically what we do with our lives is part of God's project, which is called creation.

So, to begin with, the notion of living in God's time conveys the belief that our lives are created. Referring to the biblical story of creation, one might say that "empty time" is what the author of Genesis 1 named *tohu wabohu*, "the sound and the fury," which Martin Buber and Franz Rosenzweig, in their *Verdeutschung* of the Hebrew Bible, magnificently render as "Irrsal und Wirrsal." It is time without order, without a distinction between chaos and cosmos.[3] To be created means that God made the world a place to dwell in — not just an empty space — in which time evolves between promise and fulfillment. Created time is ordered by God's providence. It is not just empty time that evolves as an endless sea of random events. The Christian theological tradition has articulated this belief in the notion of a divine economy, a space and time well ordered within which human life can flourish.

The notion of a divine economy can thus be explored as a theological antidote to the view that the fullness of our lives is of our own making. Divine economy implies the plenitude of God's goodness; in contrast, because of the assumption of empty time, the globe faces the barren consequences of an unbounded *human* economy. Within this economy, defined as an economy of scarcity, human activity is nowhere fundamentally at rest. On the contrary, it is geared up "24/7," because to be at rest is to lose opportunity. The human economy of scarcity is in pursuit of fulfilling an infinite demand that has no other measure than its own growth.

Challenging the importance of subjective time in the sense as explained, then, involves the theological notion of a divine economy. Within the divine economy, it is our vocation to respond to what we have received

---

3. I am aware that this way of phrasing it may suggest a doctrine of creation as divine form shaping unformed matter, which the church countered with its teaching of a *creatio ex nihilo*, but this is not my intention, nor is it the point at issue here. That point is to introduce the primacy of God's action as it speaks through the notion of a divine economy.

out of the plenitude of God's goodness. Thus it is the opposite of an order of economic necessity within which our main business is to achieve the greatest possible growth of wealth, both individually and collectively, under the conditions of scarcity.

In view of this project — the project of a "global economy" — there is hardly a more radical contrast imaginable than the existence of profoundly disabled human beings. Their lives could not be more different from what our popular culture portrays as a successful life. In this capacity of radical difference, the presence of profoundly disabled human beings is a countercultural force that is powerful precisely in its fragility. I suggest that, approached in these terms, the lives of profoundly disabled human beings may be taken as a sign.

Teachers

In what follows I will explore the possibility of reading this sign in view of Jesus' teaching about the lilies of the field found in the Gospel of Matthew. The lilies represent a sign of what living in God's time is. I will argue that the unexamined lives of people with profound disabilities are just such a sign. As a sign, their lives also can teach us something about what it means to live in God's time. The lilies have their own way of knowing God.

According to the Gospel of Matthew, Jesus tells his friends not to worry about tomorrow (Matt. 6:25-34). He tells them to look at the birds in the sky and the lilies of the field: they don't worry about what they will eat or how they will be clothed, Jesus says, and yet God feeds the birds and clothes the lilies. If this is what he does for them, why not trust that he would do even more for us? "Your heavenly Father knows that you need all these things. But strive first for the kingdom of God and his righteousness, and all these things will be given to you as well" (Matt. 6:32b-34).

In one of his essays, Søren Kierkegaard reflects on these words as a teaching of how to be content with the fact of being human, without any qualification. He introduces the subject in exact analogy to the question we have posed in this book: What can we learn from people with disabilities? This is apparent in the prayer with which he begins, and is worth quoting in full:

Father in heaven! From you come only good and perfect gifts. It must also be beneficial to comply with the counsel and teaching of whomever you have appointed as a teacher of human beings, as a counselor to the worried. Grant, then, that the one who is worried may truly learn from the divinely appointed teachers: the lilies in the field and the birds of the air. Amen. (Kierkegaard 1993, 157)

The lilies appear as a gift to teach us something about our being worried. Given my earlier characterization of profoundly disabled human beings, the analogy will be apparent. Our society designates some people as "profoundly disabled" because they cannot take care of themselves, among other things. They cannot take responsibility for their own lives; they could not survive even a single day out in the world on their own. The condition of being impaired in their development leaves them no alternative but to receive their lives as a gift. In view of Jesus' teaching in Matthew 6, this condition puts them on a par with the lilies in the field. They exist in an analogous way, which provides us with the possibility, I suggest, of regarding them similarly as divinely appointed teachers. It is because of this analogy that I propose to follow Kierkegaard in his reading of the Gospel of Matthew (Perkins 2005).

"Don't Worry"

Kierkegaard sets out to explain to his flock what there is to be learned from the lilies by focusing on the notion of being worried, because it is to those who are worried that the gospel is addressed, he says. Usually people who are worried about their lives resent being told that they must have faith and be strong, Kierkegaard acknowledges, because such words are often spoken by those who consider themselves strong and faithful. Consequently, those who are told not to worry are left behind with two problems instead of one: in addition to being worried, they now feel bad about themselves as well. When such is the case, Kierkegaard argues, it is a blessing to be comforted without implicit reproach or judgment (Kierkegaard 1993, 160). It is very rare to be comforted in such a way, he says, but it can be found. It can be found particularly when we behold the lilies of the field and the birds of the sky. They neither reproach nor judge. Their comfort is not covert criticism.

Having thus set the stage, Kierkegaard inserts a psychological reflection that is key to his understanding of Jesus' teaching. When people speak to comfort others, he says, there is always an implicit admonition: "Be like me!" "Do like me!" "Believe like me!" (Kierkegaard 1993, 161). For example, when Job's friends come to comfort him in his misery, they do so by telling him what they themselves would do, thus admonishing the person in agony to compare his fate with theirs. Even Job himself looks on his misery by comparing it to other people's good fortune. Kierkegaard says that the nature of human being is such that our worries reside precisely in making such comparisons. Worry is intensified by envy.

"Mind the lilies of the field, how they grow. They don't work. They don't spin," Jesus tells his friends. Even though they are beautifully dressed, they are not worried about their clothing; they don't even care. Yet they are more beautifully dressed than King Solomon. People usually worry because of comparing themselves to others. The exception to this rule is found in small children, who are in a sense like the lilies and the birds, Kierkegaard declares, because they don't judge; they are just present.

I do not mean to imply that people with profound disabilities are to be viewed as small children, but they have in common with children this feature that Kierkegaard points to. Like the lilies and the birds, they do not compare themselves with others. They do not consider their own fate in view of that of others. There is an unreflective awareness about them that enables them simply to be, without measuring themselves by measuring others. In explaining how the lilies and the birds may become our teachers, Kierkegaard points to this characteristic: they do not compare, and that is how they may become our teachers (Kierkegaard 1993, 161-62). We will not be able to really see the lilies of the field, he argues, unless we know how to be content with ourselves. This is the notion that Kierkegaard wants to explore: "In this discourse, then, let us consider how by properly looking at the lilies in the field and at the birds of the air the worried person learns to be contented with being a human being" (Kierkegaard 1993, 162). The lilies and the birds are content with themselves as they are. That is what we can learn from them.

Kierkegaard illustrates his point poetically with a parable of a mockingbird who visits a wonderful lily every day, and every day he speaks in admiration of other radiant lilies. Listening to all these praises, the lily starts to wonder what is wrong with her; she even begins to question whether she may count as a lily at all. That lily is like a human being, Kierkegaard says, and the bird mocking her is our habit of making comparisons with other people because of the belief that diversity is what matters. Imagining ourselves in the position of other people, in different times and places, is a habit that is the source of all worries.

In the worry of comparison, the worried person finally goes so far that because of diversity he forgets that he is a human being, in despair regards himself as so different from other people that he even regards himself as different from what it is to be human, just as the lily was believed to be so unimpressive that it became a question whether it actually was a lily. (Kierkegaard 1993, 169).

So what does the worried person to whom the gospel addresses itself learn from the lilies? "He learns to be contented with being a human being and not be worried about diversity among human beings" (Kierkegaard 1993, 170). He learns to speak just as solemnly and inspiringly about being human as the gospel speaks solemnly and inspiringly about the lily. This is reflected in the way we speak at solemn occasions — such as the moment of someone's death — when all talk of diversity is abolished. We speak of the human being as "the highest term of address" because, to be addressed as a human being, one "is not lower than the diversities but is raised above them," which indicates "the essentially equal glory among all human beings" (Kierkegaard 1993, 171).[4]

Freedom and Providence

Looking at other people and comparing our situation to theirs is the source of our worries, so Kierkegaard has said, but now he has to face the fact that not all our worries originate from comparison. There are daily

---

4. Kierkegaard's comments here throw a fresh light on the postmodern celebration of "diversity." Even though the latter has its primary source in epistemology, it is nonetheless remarkable that what Kierkegaard wants us to understand is a critique of "the morbid knowledge of diversity" (Kierkegaard 1993, 169). "The little bird is the poet, the seducer, or the poetic and the seductive in the human being. The poetic is like the bird's talk, true and untrue, fiction and truth. It is indeed true that there is diversity and that there is much to be said about it, but the poetic consists in maintaining that diversity, impassioned in despair or jubilation, is the supreme, and this is eternally false." In insisting that the human being is a human being "in exactly the same sense as the lily is a lily, absolutely in the same sense" (165), Kierkegaard implies the truth about our creatureliness as the gospel understands it. In comparing ourselves with others — which is the source of knowing diversity — we tend to forget that God is not interested in making comparisons between people. As Kierkegaard says, God wants us to be human as we are intended to be (165, 170). Theologically speaking, therefore, it is only because sameness defines humans as *coram deo* and as such precedes human diversity that the latter can be celebrated (Reinders 2008, 283-87).

concerns in people's lives that simply have to be met, such as food and clothing. Jesus' teaching acknowledges this, but he adds that our heavenly Father knows we need these things — so again, there is no reason to worry. "Watch the birds in the sky, they don't sow, they don't reap, they don't collect their food in barns."

Kierkegaard anticipates the skeptical response that this is fine for the birds in the sky, who live unaware of time, but responsible people do not live without temporality's foresight. "The person of foresight on earth learns from time to use time, and when he has his barn full from a past time and is provided for in the present time, he still takes care to sow seed so that he can have his barn full again in a future time" (Kierkegaard 1993, 172). While this response suggests how time underlies foresight, Kierkegaard continues, Jesus in Matthew responds very differently: "And yet your heavenly Father feeds them."

The industriousness of human foresight notwithstanding, what we learn from looking at the birds is that they are fed and are cared for by their Creator, and this tells us something about how we are cared for. The point is not that we have no responsibility for earning a living, but rather that there is no reason to be worried about these things. Here again, worry is related to comparison and diversity, as opposed to our being content with what we have received from the Father. This happens, for example, when we notice that some people are very poorly provided for, which — if one wants to escape their kind of misery — is a reason for making provisions for oneself.

To illustrate what he has in mind, Kierkegaard inserts another parable (Kierkegaard 1993, 174-77). Imagine a wild pigeon, he says, that lives in a forest, but watches how a tame pigeon living on a farm is waiting for the farmer's wagon to return from the field loaded with corn. When it arrives, the tame pigeon begins industriously storing its own share of the crop. Even though the forest provides the wild pigeon with all the food it needs, it envies the tame pigeon and tells itself that a secured livelihood on a farm must be a much better way of life than living in the dangerous forest. So it joins the tame pigeon to share in its abundance. Unfortunately, the farmer catches and kills the wild pigeon for his own sustenance.

In this parable, Kierkegaard explains, the abundance of food for the tame pigeon becomes the object of desire for the wild pigeon, even though it does not need it. In this regard it acts like the human being who attempts to secure her own existence in comparison with that of others. She wants to secure her existence, which will put an end to her freedom, as it did with the wild pigeon. To give up freedom of worry in exchange for security is to forget that it is our heavenly Father who feeds us, Kierkegaard argues. Being tempted by this exchange, people often are forgetful of the fact that a creature can no more secure its own existence than it can create itself. Only when they forget this do people begin to worry about their lives. That is when they lose sight of divine assistance. If a human being is unwilling to be content with the fact that she is a human being who is cared for by the Father, she will want to secure her own existence. But, Kierkegaard wants to know, what is the something more that the discontented human being wants?

> The something more is: to be himself his own providence for all his life or perhaps merely for tomorrow; and if that is what he wants, then he walks — cunningly — into the snare, the wealthy as well as the poor. Thus he wants to entrench himself, so to speak, in a little or large area where he will not be the object of God's providence and the supporting care of the heavenly Father. He may not perceive, before it is too late, that in this entrenched security he is living — in a prison. (Kierkegaard 1993, 178)

The desire to be free from worry, "to be his own providence," brings about precisely what human beings seek to avoid. There is no security but only imprisonment to be gained from human concern when he forgets that he is created. Human beings cannot secure their own lives. Here again, Kierkegaard concludes, it appears that our unfreedom stems from comparison. When humans aspire to be the source of their own freedom — that is, to be like God — this is when they find themselves incarcerated.

Divine Economy

In his book *Wie Geschöpfe Leben*, the German theologian Hans G. Ulrich has taken up Kierkegaard's Lutheran sensibilities about *Sorge* in his reflections about the connection between the divine and the human economy. In fact, Ulrich traces Kierkegaard's discussion back to a distinction in Luther between two kinds of concerns: one is the concern to have our needs fulfilled; the other is the concern to secure our own existence (Ulrich 2005, 347, 360-65). The gospel promises that concern about our own existence is met by God's gracious gift of salvation in Jesus Christ. There is no reason to worry about what will become of us, because God has delivered us from the abyss of existential worry ("abgründiger Lebenssorge"). In Luther's eyes, that is what salvation is. Consequently, Luther argues, human beings are free from worrying about themselves, and thus they can turn to their calling of living as God's creatures in the divine economy.

Ulrich's analysis is particularly sensitive to secular concepts of human economy that include this existential dimension by suggesting that all our needs, material and immaterial, can be met by economic activity. Not only must economic activity fail to fulfill this promise, but the very thought of that already signals a forgetfulness about human creatureliness (Ulrich 2005, 350-56). That economic activity fails to fill the existential void is shown, according to Ulrich, by the fact that capitalist production only brings an ever-expanding demand for growth. Economic activity cannot fulfill human destiny because fulfilling human destiny cannot be secured within secular time.[5] Moreover, it blocks from view what human beings should be concerned with, namely, living together according to God's righteousness. Sharing the divine economy is not about the production of goods — material and immaterial — but about righteousness toward the neighbor.

In this connection, Matthew 6 also has a prominent place in Ulrich's thought. To be worried about our own existence, whatever form it takes, is to ignore the primacy of God's action. "Do not worry" entails the promise that God will provide. Those who ignore the primacy of God's action seek to secure for themselves "a place where God's providence has nothing to do," as Kierkegaard puts it. This does not mean, of course, that it does not matter what humans do, but that whatever they do, their prime responsibility is to listen to what it means to be God's creatures. According to Ulrich, this is what Jesus means when he tells his disciples, "You first attend his kingdom and his righteousness, and all this [food and clothing] will be given to you" (Matt. 6:33). Our worldly wisdom usually has this the other way around: while we strive for the things we need for our security, the kingdom will come as a gift. Industrious people usually think it wiser to follow their own order of priorities and not to let their hope for treasures in heaven get in the way of accumulating treasures on earth.[6]

5. In this connection, Ulrich points to Heidegger's notion of "Dasein als Sorge" (Ulrich 2005, 360), which is to suggest that there is a dimension of want in human *existence* that cannot be fulfilled without denying that it is a dimension of *human* existence.

6. Ulrich quotes Luther: "Es ist aber der leidige Unglaube allzeit im Wege, dass Gott solche Werke nicht in uns wirken kann und wir sie nicht erfahren noch erkennen kön-

Heavenly Wisdom

In view of Matthew 6:25-34, it appears that worldly and heavenly wisdom are evidently at cross purposes with one another. Jesus is clearly not endorsing anything like the Western way of using time as a commodity — that much is clear. To the extent that our economy is domesticated by worldly wisdom, Jesus' teaching falsifies the ubiquitous notion that "time is money." For time to be money, it must be conceived of as a scarce commodity in the possession of which human beings are able to carry out their plans and projects in competition with others (see Hauerwas, chap. 9 above). If time is money, then there must be profit in selling it. In that case, there is no time to be wasted, which indicates how an economy of scarcity creates a need for carrying out our plans and projects in the most cost-effective way.

Heavenly wisdom teaches us differently. Time cannot be money because the days of our lives are God's gift. Since we are his creatures, we live in God's time. The notion of God's time indicates that whatever we think must be done, will be done as a response to what has been received. There can be no sharper contrast with this insight than exists in the notion of time as money. The very notion of time as money indicates how secular conceptions of economic activity may in fact end in imprisonment by our own doing. "Man desires to be his own providence," Kierkegaard says, and that desire is premised by the belief that we need to secure our own future. This belief forgets the fact that securing a future for itself is not the prime responsibility of human action; the prime responsibility of human action is in our freedom to receive the gift of God's friendship (Reinders 2008).

In view of the worldly wisdom discussed in Kierkegaard's essay, people with profound disabilities have absolutely nothing to say for themselves. They lose out in every comparison. They know of no plans or projects; they do not know how to secure a living for themselves; they could not even find a single meal to feed themselves. Nonetheless, there is something to be learned from them, as is true of the lilies of the field and the birds of the sky. They behave as creatures in the true sense of the word in that they are not concerned with their needs because of a comparison with other be-

---

nen. Wir wollen satt sein und aller Dinge genug haben, ehe der Hunger und die Notdurft kommt, und versorgen uns mit Vorrat auf zukünftigen Hunger und Notdurft. Was ist das für ein Glaube, der da Gott trauet, solange du Vorrat fühlst und weit, wie du dir helfen kannst?" (Ulrich 2005, 363).

ings, as the unhappy lily and the wild pigeon in Kierkegaard's parables were. Instead, they are content with what they are. The reason, Jesus' teaching suggests, is that they know how to receive God's abundant gifts. In contrast, people in the business of securing their own future apparently do not know what it is to receive. At any rate, they don't want to be dependent on it. In following the wisdom of human economy, they necessarily replace the primacy of God's action with that of their own.

Secular Time

In the concept of our worldly wisdom, then, our time is secular time. Secular time is structured by how human action shapes the world. In structuring what they do, people create the meaning of time through their objectives and achievements. This explains why many of our contemporaries seem to believe that "meaning" is what they produce by their own action (Reinders 2000). As I have argued earlier, the default position of this concept must be that secular time is essentially empty. As such, it necessarily becomes controlled time within which human activity is securing its own existence by producing material and immaterial goods, and life becomes valuable and meaningful when we are in the possession of these goods. As long as we can "give" meaning to our lives, we are in control of our existence. From the perspective of worldly wisdom, the lack of control equals the loss of meaning.

In contrast, living in the divine economy prioritizes God's action, which means that living in God's time is necessarily characterized by a lack of control. That is why Jesus tells his people that they should be expecting the kingdom at an unexpected hour, just as servants should stay awake for the coming of their master at an unpredictable hour, like a thief in the night (Luke 12:35-40). We have no control over the kingdom by planning industrious action; but expecting the kingdom, rather than industrious action, is the goal of our lives. What we are called to do is to prepare the way for its coming by responding to God's gifts.

I trust that this analogy between the lilies of the field and the birds in the sky and profoundly disabled human beings existing beyond subjective time as our teachers has been illuminating. To fully explain the logic of this analogy, I should note that in Matthew 6, Jesus uses the rabbinic rule of *qal wachomer*, which is the logic of reasoning from what is "smaller" to what is "greater." So the argument says: "If this is true for the birds and the lilies, how much more must it be true for you" (Matt. 6:31). Without implying a relationship of superiority, we can learn an important lesson from people with profound disabilities precisely in this respect.[7] More than most of us — readers and writers of texts, let us say — these human beings manage to do what the lilies and the birds do. There is no other way of being for them than just to be as they are, so that their existence cannot but exemplify a fundamental trust that God will provide. There is no way to secure their existence for themselves, which means there is no way of existing for them other than to trust the goodness of life as it comes. This is what the gospel's analogy teaches: living in trust that the Father will give what we need is living in his presence, here and now. Human beings with profound disability are a sign to us in that they exemplify living that kind of life. When seen in this light, their lives may appear as beacons of hope — in the sense intended by Matthew and Kierkegaard — rather than as markers of meaninglessness.

As a final personal note, these reflections evoke a question that never fails to intrigue me. Could we say, without intending to reinstall the medieval tradition of "holy innocents," that because of the unreflective immediacy of their existence here and now, profoundly disabled human beings are somehow closer to God's presence? Jesus certainly did not maintain high expectations of our ability to trust God: "You of little faith!" he scornfully addressed his followers, seeing how they were busy securing a livelihood for themselves (Luke 12:28) — as opposed to being prepared to trust whatever God gives at the moment he wants to give it. If there is anything to be learned from profoundly disabled human beings, I think, it is their embodied way of existing as a matter of trust, without control over their own lives. This is what it truly means to live in God's time.

References

Harris, J. 1985. *The value of life: Introduction to medical ethics.* London: Routledge, 1985.

Kierkegaard, S. 1993. What we learn from the lilies in the field and from the birds of the air. In *Upbuilding discourses in various spirits,* ed. and trans. H. V. Hong and E. H. Hong, 155-212. Princeton: Princeton University Press.

7. The relationship between "smaller" and "greater" is not one of superiority but of responsibility. Jesus is saying to us that if the lilies and the birds have no problem relying on divine providence, how much more reason do we have to do the same.

Perkins, R. L., ed. 2005. *Upbuilding discourses in various spirits.* International Kierkegaard Commentary, vol. 15. Atlanta: Mercer University Press.

Reinders, H. S. 2000. 'The meaning of life' in liberal society. In *Meaningful care: A multidisciplinary approach to the meaning of care for people with mental retardation,* ed. J. Stolk, T. A. Boer, and R. Seldenrijk, 65-84. Dordrecht: Kluwer.

————. 2007. Life's goodness: On disability, genetics, and 'choice.' In *Theology, disability and the new genetics: Why science needs the church,* ed. J. Swinton and B. Brock, 163-81. London: T. & T. Clark.

————. 2008. *Receiving the gift of friendship: Profound disability, theological anthropology, and ethics.* Grand Rapids: Eerdmans.

Ulrich, H. G. 2005. *Wie Geschöpfe leben: Konturen evangelischer Ethik.* Münster: LIT Verlag.

Chapter Thirteen

On the Importance of Suffering:
The Paradoxes of Disability

CHRISTOPHER NEWELL

A Moment of Suffering

"I want to die," I sobbed to my wife. It is hardly an unusual sentiment for me. Tears streamed down my cheeks. The demands of life were too great. It is tough enough just surviving every day with disability, let alone the requirements to be amazingly amazing, to endure barriers and prejudice and the unconscious social norms that create disability. On top of this there are the realities of pain, the impact of drugs, the hypoxia that changes my mood, and the mind-numbing exhaustion. The privatization of disability was happening so profoundly.

Yet the context was hardly exceptional. I am someone who uses oxygen and related respiratory therapy daily, as well as a wheelchair for mobility. Impaired bones, muscles, and especially a deteriorating spine that requires the use of morphine and other drugs that cloud the mind markedly these days. All of this combined with a set of lungs that have been damaged and struggling ever since I was born. Over my life I have had many years of hospitalization (almost dying a variety of times) and the experience of failing at school. My younger years were capped off with the joy of assembling refresher towel sets for a fast-food company in a sheltered workshop at the age of eighteen. While I do not use medical disease labels in this essay deliberately, because in my experience medical labeling can be oppressive, it is clear that, for many, such a personal history as mine attests to the tragedy of disability. Yet the reason for my wanting to die was far more than any individual pathology. The essays

assembled in this volume help us embrace a far more complex understanding.

As I sought to journey from Tasmania to France to join the conference
in Trosly-Breuil, just about every possible difficulty precluded my writing
a paper. I was faced once again with an insensitive airline that required yet
more medical certificates for oxygen supply, while making statements
about what I could and could not do without referring to me. Exhausted
by trying to catch up after the realities of hospitalization, I was struggling
with teaching requirements and deadlines, particularly for this essay,
which was already very late. I felt it was too much.

Despite this, as the L'Arche community embraced me, so too did the
scholars in this book, whose writing richly suggests an embrace of myself
as someone with impairment. Reflecting on this experience, I came to realize a deeper dimension to my suffering. As someone who has struggled to
belong to the academic community, I am aware of profound and confusing
paradoxes in my life. I have published extensively in critiquing the biomedical model (e.g., Goggin and Newell 2005). At the same time, however,
I need the developments of medicine and science to keep me alive and
functioning in a deteriorating body. I am aware of the importance in my
life of accepting the limitations of my body and the realities of pain, but
yet I work in an academic context where the expectation is to transcend
limitation and "publish or perish." Weakness is not an option.

Listening

I have to reveal these personal experiences to the reader to account for why
I did not want to write this paper. I certainly did not want to write it in the
way I have. To be honest, I wanted to offer a scholarly academic paper
about what we can learn from "the disabled" that showed no traces of my
own experience. Some months prior to the conference in Trosly (which
was the origin of the essays in this book), I asked an Australian L'Arche
community representative if he could come up with a narrative from the
community with which I could start — something on which I could safely
pronounce. It turned out that my request was prioritized very low, which
was probably due to the daily struggles that people with disabilities face.
Presumably, they had more urgent things to do.

So finding myself without "a narrative," I faced the question of what
we have to learn from people with disabilities. I decided to focus on what it

is to listen, and I realized that there was much for me to learn, which was attested to by Miriam-Rose Ungunmerr-Baumann, an aboriginal elder from Daly River in Australia, who articulates an Australian spiritual foundation for listening. She talks of spirituality in the following way, and thus about a basis for my listening:

> What I want to talk about is a special quality of my people. I believe it is the most important. It is our most unique gift. It is perhaps the greatest gift we can give to our fellow Australians. In our language this quality is called Dadirri.
>
> Dadirri is an inner, deep listening and quiet, still awareness. Dadirri recognizes the deep spring that is inside us. We call on it and it calls to us. This is the gift that Australia is thirsting for. It is something like what you call "contemplation." A big part of Dadirri is listening.
>
> In our Aboriginal way, we learned to listen from our earliest days. We could not live good or useful lives unless we listened. This was the normal way for us to learn — not by asking questions. We learnt by watching and listening, waiting and then acting. Our people have passed this way of listening for over 40,000 years. My people are not threatened by silence. They are completely at home with it.
>
> They have lived for thousands of years with Nature's quietness. My people today recognize and experience in this quietness the great Life-giving Spirit, the Father of us all. We all have to try to listen to the God within us, to our own country and to one another. Our culture is different. We are asking our fellow Australians to take time to know us; to be still and to listen to us. (quoted in Crotty 1998, 65).

Reflecting on these words made me aware of the importance of my own narrative as someone who experienced so much difficulty in getting to a conference that I wanted to join. I realized that my task in getting there was not so much to make an "academic" contribution, but to offer, as Jean Vanier so graciously suggests, an account of what overwhelmed me, as a person with a disability — my own suffering. In reflecting on my vulnerability, I believe I have a contribution to make.

In exploring the experience of suffering, I recognize a deep feeling of spiritual isolation. The therapeutic for me was provided by being able to sob in the arms of a wife who knew I mattered, who thought I belonged to the world. Given a choice between 20 mg. of IV morphine and a hug, I know the latter is more therapeutic but is denied to so many. The scholarship found in the papers in this book — offered in a most remarkable environment of embrace, L'Arche — also provides me with an intellectual embrace that suggests there is time and place within the academy for deeply listening to people with disability.

Suffering and Biotechnology

Suffering is a central aspect of how many societies view disability. Ideas about suffering have long histories in religion, ethics, and health care, especially in the conception of living that elusive goal — the good life. We are only too aware of how religious accounts and indigenous knowledge were displaced by the rise of Enlightenment ideas within which science and technology were portrayed as ends in themselves. Crucial in these ideas, particularly as they play out in the narration of biomedical science, was the elimination of suffering. This has not changed in our post-Enlightenment culture. In its modern form, biomedical science conceives of disability as the epitome of suffering, an exemplary tragedy located within the individual, sometimes regarded even as a form of living death. That is why biotechnology is regarded as a highly desirable way of dealing with fear of disability, and in turn, of suffering.

In this respect, I see the genetic revolution as premised on the idea that humanity should be delivered from disability. Disability and its correlate, suffering, shapes the development of genetics as well as the reemergence of eugenics in the name of "therapy" (Lynn 2001). I see debates regarding stem cells and the cures these techniques promise in the same light. In public debates regarding stem cells that have been conducted in Australia and New Zealand, I can but note the centrality of disability, but also the almost invariably marginal presence of people with disabilities as participants in these debates. The singular exception may be found in the role of figures promoting a miracle cure, unable to accept disability, such as the broken Superman, Christopher Reeve (Goggin and Newell 2005).

Again, with respect to other biotechnologies, there are two associated discourses at work here: one predicating "suffering," the other predicating "therapy." A key assumption in these discourses is that biotechnology will deliver us from the suffering found in disability. Central to all of these is the presupposition of disability as the antithesis of freedom. Looking at these discourses, I suggest that society avoids the exploration of contradictions between the ends of health care, disability policy, biotechnology, and

theology. I find little imagination as to how these disciplines might inter-
sect. The essays in this book may help us rethink the links between technology and policy and disability in view of the diverging conceptions of
the good life they embody.

The Context of Suffering

I have rigorously, all of my life, avoided talking about disability in terms of
suffering. So why would I now want to turn to look at that? The last two
years have been particularly important. Having spent literally years of my
life in hospitals with a variety of painful, distressing, and seemingly dehumanizing treatments, these last two years have included many months of
hospitalization with breakthrough spinal pain and complications. Contrary to the theoretical account of the social model of disability (Shakespeare 2006), locating disability as constructed by society, the long rehabil-
itation and new high doses of painkillers and other drugs have led me to
realize that I can no longer deny it: there is an important dimension of suffering to disability, even though not all disabilities are necessarily about
suffering. However, this dimension exceeds the experience of physical and
mental pain; there are many social and spiritual aspects of suffering. This I
came to realize as I struggled with the multiple travel arrangements associated with my dangerous body.

It is important we realize how dangerous the disabled body is.
Traveling in increasingly rigorous security arrangements, I came to realize
how the disabled body really is a form of terrorism. There is a war on terror that is long established, of course, which we call "therapy," embodied in
medicine as a profession, with its ennobling duty of care, or even love. It is
a dangerous war for people with disabilities, however, within which even
the notion of Christian love, or *agape,* may turn into a threat, as, for example, in Joseph Fletcher's account of it (Fletcher 1979). Within the context of
the underlying project of modernity, largely unexamined, the dominant
social approaches to disability reveal that our able-bodied culture does not
want to know about human finiteness and mortality. Within the context of
that project, which defines the context of suffering in our society, disability
appears as the dangerous "other" in the form of terror on wheels, and on
crutches, and most disturbingly in a world where intellect is all, in the
form of a disturbed mind.

We may also realize that disability is a contested and paradoxical sociopolitical space. As I have indicated earlier, I was once a clear advocate of a social account of the oppression of people with impairments, focusing on prejudice and injustice rather than on disabling bodies. Yet, increasingly for many of us, the realities of nonstatic and deteriorating impairment cannot be denied. But this paradoxical nature also creates a space of reflection and exchange. In this connection, the experience of suffering and even needless discrimination has helped me learn as a human being — and as a priest and academic. In my first lecture to entering medical students, I reflect on the possibility that when they graduate, I will be a patient of theirs who expresses a desire to die. It has happened before to former students of mine, and it will happen again. Therefore, I cannot be an aloof professor with them; instead, such an admission of shared humanity and pain calls them into relationship with me. Likewise, I offer this dissonant essay in a different voice from so many others in this collection; I offer it honestly within the difficulties I have decided to acknowledge.

I have come to realize not only that brokenness is important, but also that I really have something to offer to humanity: that is, to reflect on the projects of bioethics and theology, a reflection that comes from an experience of the very attributes of disability that are feared by the people carrying out such projects, including myself. The real question is not whether, but *how* brokenness will be valued. Despite all the important work of theologians such as Nouwen and Vanier, as well as the central role of brokenness in the crucifixion narrative and the Gospels in general, embracing it still seems to be, theologically, a step too far.[1] A major challenge to us, in listening to people with disability, is to have room for narratives such as this, and to create space for those narratives to help repair the social situations we find so normal (Nelson 2001).

I am also mindful, remembering Miriam-Rose Ungunmerr-Baumann's remarks on silence, that for all that the writers in this collection of essays have written about the insights found in and of disability, there is also a need to create a space so that we may listen to the *still* voice of those with disability. Not only our lives and bodies, but also even a lack of voice and communication capacity, may speak so loudly. Otherwise, those who live without life-limiting impairment speak *about* rather than listen and be *with*. Part of the cultural context of suffering is the ubiquitous tendency to

---

1. Jean Vanier is, of course, one of the contributors to this volume, and I allow his essay here to speak for itself. With regard to the work of Henri Nouwen, see esp. Nouwen, *The Wounded Healer: Ministry in Contemporary Society* (New York: Doubleday, 1972).

worry about its adequate representation rather than actually allowing it to be present.

In addition, I realize that the realities of suffering mean I have to focus on some real basics in life, that is, daily encountering my finite mortality. It is one thing to be wise enough to recognize that getting up and getting dressed can be an achievement in itself; it is quite another thing, however, to be comfortable and at peace with myself in doing so. Yet suffering particularly occurs when I reorient myself to the ways of the world, within which a professional paper not written and delivered in time makes me become a failure yet again. Combined with all the other challenges I have to face, a wish to die reflects a perceived lack of virtue as well as a hatred for the very body with which I am usually so comfortable.

This is why community and relationship have something profound to offer me, which I was reminded of by the experience of participating in the conference at L'Arche. I found the experience of listening to, and participating in, the dialectic of this temporary academic community to be holistic healing and a balm to the soul. The many reasons for my suffering are not a lack of morphine, or of therapy, but a lack of relationship. I wept when I received encouraging emails from the writers of these essays. They *did* theology and acted out an ethic of embrace when it all seemed too difficult for me to get to Trosly. I was embraced in conversation and at table. It is in response to what this gift of community means that I weep when I encounter a theology that grips me in embrace. This experience accounts for an ethic that does not reluctantly claim my life simply as precious, but claims my life as inherently dignified. It is an ethic that does not shy away from me, or from the awkwardness of my voice, but reaches for God — in the very places we all fear. This lived gift of a theology of the dignity of the human person ultimately is required when so many secular accounts create indignity.

The Paradoxes of Disability

Yet for all this, my life and the lives of people with disability are paradoxical, and this is found in bioethical debates. Certainly when we think about it, contemporary bioethical and spiritual dimensions of life may be examined in terms of suffering, which is central to the narration of health, religion, normalcy, and the comparatively recent discipline of which I am part, bioethics. The paradoxes of disability are fascinating: on the one hand, I find that I grow through the experience of adversity; on the other hand, there is no way in which I can wish to cultivate any more "character-forming moments." A character-forming moment is when all of life is chaotic and my world seems to be ending.

It is in the beginning and end of life that we find those paradoxes most clearly (Post and Gaventa, chaps. 2 and 8 above). In the debates regarding euthanasia, I find that disability has much to teach us. As someone who has requested death at the hands of a medical professional, I will always be grateful for a response that asked me for my reaons. The binary logic in euthanasia debates seems to allow nothing of the muckiness of life that is experienced by so many of us, certainly the muckiness of life as a person with disability. What I find very sad is that certain church organizations and right-to-life groups are quick to pick up on issues that people such as me have raised regarding the threat of the lives of people with disabilities. Yet they do not routinely offer relationship in community; and it is because of the absence of community that so many of us want to die.

While many faith traditions and church organizations provide services to people with disability, the way most of those services are provided helps to reinforce a negative account of disability, according to which it is thought that these people have a low quality of life. There is a lack of critical engagement in addressing the role of both medical and charitable discourse. This lack suggests to me that ultimately these organizations tend to benefit from talking about, rather than listening to, those who are identified as having a disability. In this regard, the L'Arche community is different: its setting of embrace — within which the present papers were given — embodies a profound critique of merely providing professional services and responses. It is time for the pious utterances *about* people with disability to stop. The meeting at Trosly was a tangible attempt to address the structural and ideological reasons for the neglect experienced by people with impairments.

As we listen to the voices of what causes suffering, there is much more than the physiological. For me to know that I am other — outside of the nice, normal, and natural — and that the church and theology as a project has largely failed to address this exacerbates and makes unbearable any physiological symptoms that I might have. What a wonderful turnaround it would be if the insights of the essays in this book were used to shape theology and social policy that seeks to use the experience of disability in seeking to examine and claim the good life. This would help address cultural assumptions that the good life is the (largely) unexamined antithesis of disability. So many essays in this collection address this powerfully.

Likewise, when we examine those controversial issues having to do with selective abortion and genetic screening on grounds of so-called medical conditions, we then examine some very important issues of *lived values*. The interventions offered in the context of biotechnology are predominantly based on the avoidance of suffering. As a parent, I know that I would do almost anything to avoid having my child experience pain. Yet, despite all the pain, discomfort, and life-threatening challenges to my being over the years, I would not immediately take a miracle cure tomorrow. The person that I am has learned so much from the very experiences I knew — and know — to be negative. And I now find — paradoxically and disturbingly so — that these situations have been a positive. I think that I am a much better person, priest, and academic for the very experiences that I would have done almost anything to avoid. This is not an argument to rush out and get a disability tomorrow, of course. But it is one to make us think, to stop, to pause, and in such a space as this to allow us to hear the deeply disturbing voices that call into question our social values.

There is no better example of our lived social values than in the increased targeting of Down syndrome around the world. The power relations dominating the discourses on disability are apparent in that people with Down syndrome, who say that they are pleased to be who they are, are largely ignored as society seeks to find the technical fix for suffering. Somehow or other, our social institutions and discourse always seem to forget to ask what suffering really involves and what it is to be normal.

Creating Disability

Accordingly, as I reflect on suffering and its sociocultural context, I cannot help but reflect that theology and the church have much to offer to the broader society when they manage to listen to people with disabilities. At any rate, people with disabilities have much to offer to the church and theology, particularly in its academic form. Sadly, in most places around the world, people with disabilities do not experience this interest in listening. I certainly cannot relate to an abstract God casting lots with my life. For me, suffering is crucial to the narration of what it is to be a Christian because, within the broken incarnate God, I find the particular attributes essential for upholding and embracing my life and making sense of my complex journey. In particular, the centrality of the suffering of Jesus — not just in persecution during his life, death, and resurrection but also in his experience of being other — means that I can relate in a very intimate way to a very human God.

Therefore, I have come to reflect that there is an important role for suffering in shaping an authentically lived and experienced good life. My dependence on a variety of people of good will that I have never met is required every day. It requires me to swallow my pride, subjecting myself to medical certification and an enormous degree of trust. It has led me to be deeply distressed. Yet it has led me to suggest that disability is a deeply important spiritual adventure. As Frederic and Mary Ann Brussat argue:

> Life is a sacred adventure. Every day we encounter signs that point to the active presence of the Spirit in the world around us. Spiritual literacy is the ability to read the signs written in the texts of our own experiences. Whether viewed as a gift from God or a skill to be cultivated, this facility enables us to discern and decipher a world full of meaning.
>
> Spiritual literacy is practiced in all the world's wisdom traditions. Medieval Catholic monks called it "reading the book of the world." Muslims suggest that everything that happens outside and inside us is a letter to be read. Native Americans find their way through the wilderness by "reading signs." From ancient times to today, spiritually literate people have been able to locate within their daily life points of connection with the sacred. (Brussat and Brussat 1996, 15)

Conclusion: The Importance and Difficulties of Suffering

In these essays we see disability as involving suffering, but as far more than suffering. Disability is crucial to understanding life, to understanding normalcy, and to transforming bioethics and theology. Healing found in brokenness and community, when suffering may still be present, is a wonderful paradox.

I long for an account of science, theology, and community that addresses and embraces the paradoxes of disability. The community of L'Arche at Trosly addresses and embraces those known to be "other." The insights of the temporary community drawn together for this group of essays are a vital way of addressing the suffering with which I started this reflection. They invite us toward a radical future: people with disability embraced within science and theology.

References

Brussat, F., and M. A. Brussat. 1996. *Spiritual lsteracy: Reading the Sacred in every-day life.* New York: Touchstone.

Crotty, E. 1998. Spirituality and justice. *Ministry, Society and Theology* 12 (2): 61-68.

Fletcher, J. 1979. *Humanhood: Essays in biomedical ethics.* New York: Prometheus.

Goggin, G., and C. Newell. 2005. *Disability in Australia: Exposing a social apartheid.* Sydney: UNSW Press.

Lynn, R. 2001. *Eugenics: A reassessment.* Westport, CT: Praeger.

Nelson, H. L. 2001. *Damaged identities, narrative repair.* Ithaca, NY: Cornell University Press.

Nouwen, H. J. M. 1972. *The wounded healer: Ministry in contemporary society.* New York: Doubleday.

Shakespeare, T. 2006. *Disability rights and wrongs.* London and New York: Routledge.

Index